PEACE WITH RUSSIA?

by

AVERELL HARRIMAN

SIMON AND SCHUSTER

NEW YORK · 1959

Contents

I	From Stalin to Khrushchev	1
II	Russia for the Russians?	9
III	The Powder Keg Myth	21
IV	The Consumer Comes Last	37
V	Khrushchev's Concrete Houses	49
VI	Stalin's Bread and Khrushchev's Butter	67
VII	More Steel	81
VIII	Terror	101
IX	Discipline	119
X	Ferment	127
XI	Circuses	149
XII	All-Out Competitive Coexistence	161

ACKNOWLEDGMENTS

Much of the material of this book was gathered during a long journey through the Soviet Union in the late spring of 1959. I would like therefore to take this opportunity to express my thanks to First Deputy Premier Anastas Mikoyan and to Georgi Zhukov, Chairman of the Committee for Cultural Relations with Foreign Countries, for their help in arranging my itinerary. I would also like to thank the scores of officials in Moscow and other cities and on the farms I visited for the hospitality and time they accorded me. I am grateful also to my numerous guides and interpreters, including Mr. Zhukov's assistant, Vasili V. Vakrushev, who accompanied me throughout my travel and contributed much to its interest.

I am also indebted to my traveling companions. My wife and Mary Russell helped greatly by their observations and comments. Charles W. Thayer contributed immeasurably through his command of the Russian language and the voluminous notes he kept of my conversations. The opinions and conclusions in this book, naturally, are entirely my own.

Finally, I must express my deep appreciation to the thousands of private Soviet citizens who welcomed us so cordially wherever we went.

A. H.

PEACE
WITH
RUSSIA?

CHAPTER ONE

From Stalin to Khrushchev

I ONCE CONFESSED to Stalin that my first visit to his country had been without visa or passport. He looked a bit startled and I hastened to explain that it had been in Czarist days, on a visit to Alaska with my father, when we had landed briefly on the coast and had been warmly greeted by some Siberian Eskimos.

"That couldn't happen now," Stalin commented confidently.

When I made that trip back in 1899, Marx's call for world revolution made fifty years before was considered a crackpot's dream. Even Marx himself had predicted that Russia, a backward agrarian country, would be among the last countries to go Communist—long after the United States.

When Russia emerged from World War I as the first Marxist state, many of the ablest political observers in Europe and America were convinced it could not survive. As late as 1926 many were still predicting that it would collapse within five years at the most. That year I went to

Moscow to find out for myself what the regime's prospects of survival were. I saw no evidence of an early collapse.

Two years before, I had joined a group to undertake a large manganese concession in the Caucasus under Lenin's New Economic Policy. During my visit I discussed the concession with several Soviet leaders, including Leon Trotsky, with whom I had a four-hour talk. I found that Trotsky had already lost his bid for Soviet leadership as successor to Lenin and that Stalin was becoming more and more firmly established in the Kremlin. Anticipating that he would reverse Lenin's policy and squeeze out all foreign concessions, I decided that we should give up the manganese mines as soon as possible. This advice my associates accepted, and we negotiated a settlement with the Soviet government under which our investment was recouped with a reasonable profit. Other concessionaires who tried to hold on were less fortunate.

But even then and in the years following between the wars, the idea of the Soviet Union's spearheading a world revolution was seldom taken seriously. The country was racked in turn by famines, by economic chaos, by a collectivization drive in which millions died, and finally by the great purges of the thirties, in which many of the best brains in the regime were liquidated. Few people imagined that the Soviet Union would ever be strong enough to lead a serious world drive for Communism once the initial postwar political confusion in the West had subsided.

Yet all through this period Stalin never lost sight of the ultimate goal—world domination by Communism. In every country where it could, the Communist Party under direction from the Kremlin attempted to stir unrest and, if possible, revolution. When the Roosevelt Administration recognized the Soviet Union, the President extracted a pledge from Soviet Foreign Minister Maxim Litvinov that the Soviet regime would not interfere in our internal affairs by means of propaganda from its Communist Party. Needless to say, the Kremlin broke that pledge within months of making it. But even then Communist Party activity was regarded in the countries of the West more as an impertinent interference and a nuisance than as a dangerous threat to our constitutional structures.

When the Germans invaded the Soviet Union in 1941, President Roosevelt sent me to Moscow on an Anglo-American mission with Lord Beaverbrook to negotiate a war-aid agreement with Stalin. In August 1942 I returned to Moscow with Prime Minister Churchill, representing the President for the first military-strategy talks with Stalin. In the autumn of 1943 I became Ambassador to the Soviet Union, and I remained there until January 1946. During this period I saw Stalin regularly—far more than any American before or since. And now I have just come home from a long trip through the Soviet Union and a series of frank talks with that nation's present leaders.

When the war ended and the Soviet Union was left as one of the two great powers, the old Marxist slogan of world revolution became a real threat. Now at last Russia had the power to conquer and hold countries beyond its frontiers in Eastern Europe and to exert powerful influences in every corner of the globe.

Even before Germany surrendered it became clear to me that the outwardly friendly relations of our wartime alliance were not going to survive the peace. I reported to the President, the Secretary of State and other members of the Cabinet that the outward thrust of Communism was not dead and that we might well have to face an ideological war against an antagonist just as vigorous and dangerous as

Nazism or Fascism. In April 1945 I cabled Washington: "We must realize that the Soviet program is the establishment of totalitarianism ending personal liberty and democracy as we know and respect it."

During one of my talks with Stalin he told me he expected Communism to flourish in "the cesspools of capitalism." The economic dislocations of liberated Western Europe were creating just such dangorous conditions even before the war ended. Referring to these areas, I wired Washington on April 4: "The Communist Party or its associates everywhere are using economic difficulties in areas under our responsibilities to promote Soviet concepts and policies and to undermine the influence of the Western Allies. The only hope of stopping Soviet penetration is the development of sound economic conditions." I recommended specifically that in addition to the relief program of UNRRA "we should through such economic aid as we can give to our Western allies, including Greece as well as Italy, re-establish a reasonable life for the people of these countries."

Two full years elapsed before the Truman Doctrine was proclaimed and aid sent first to Greece and then, through Interim Aid and finally the Marshall Plan, to Italy, France and other nations of Western Europe. Literally in the nick of time, the economic collapse Stalin had counted on was averted. Western Europe was saved from communization and its vitality and vigor were restored.

Communist ambitions were not, of course, confined to Europe. In April 1945, after President Roosevelt's death, I returned to Washington to report to President Truman and raised with members of the Cabinet a number of questions that were disturbing me deeply. While I have no personal records of these oral discussions, Secretary of the

Navy James Forrestal recorded in his diaries, which have since been published, some which he attended. He wrote that I at that time recommended a re-examination of the Yalta Agreement in view of the Soviet failure to carry out its part of that contract in Eastern Europe. I suggested that our policy toward Korea be reviewed and I raised the question of whether we wanted to destroy Japan or retain it after the war as a power in the Far East. I also raised the problem of Indochina and the possible necessity for our eventual military assistance in that area. Finally I urged that we guard against Communism in China, lest we ultimately find several hundred million Chinese ready to "march when the Kremlin ordered."

These views on the Kremlin's threat were not popular at the time. During the United Nations conference in San Francisco in May 1945, I expressed them at an off-the-record news conference. Later I was attacked in the press for being too unfriendly to our wartime ally. It was not until the Communist *coup d'état* in Czechoslovakia in February of 1948 and the Berlin Blockade a few months later that the illusion of peaceful coexistence with the Soviet Union was finally dispelled.

Recently a newspaper friend of mine reminded me that while passing through London in 1945 I had told him, "We are going to have trouble with the Soviet Union for the rest of our lives—even if we live to be a hundred."

In April of 1945 I had cabled from Moscow to Washington information Stalin had given me about his ambitious plans for Russian industrial expansion. The plan, I reported, would take fifteen or twenty years during which, among other things, Russian steel production capacity was to be tripled from the prewar level. We now know that these plans were not daydreams. Both Stalin and Khrushchev had pushed the program with the greatest vigor, and the steel capacity of which I wrote has already been tripled—in fourteen years.

This industrial expansion has raised a new kind of threat to the non-Communist world. While Stalin planned to exploit "the cesspools of capitalism" to expand Communism, Khrushchev now believes that the success of his industrial expansion with improved living standards will give him a new, powerful weapon to further Communist revolution. In one of my recent talks with him he said frankly, "We can demonstrate the advantages of our system and set an example to other countries which they will have to follow."

This concept of Communist expansion by example, Khrushchev implied, will be particularly effective in the underdeveloped countries impatient to leap from a primitive agrarian community to a self-sustaining industrial state.

Since I left the Soviet Union early in 1946 I have tried to keep abreast of the changes that have taken place there, especially since Stalin's death. I have talked to returning travelers and diplomats. I have followed the press reports and studied analyses by researchers and specialists in Soviet affairs.

These reports have revealed, it seems to me, several key problems and questions on the answers to which the future of Soviet affairs and our relations with Russia will depend. But the answers are often contradictory, sometimes confused and at times unconvincing.

Khrushchev, for example, has been alleged to be so much softer and more demagogic than Stalin that he was dissipating the Kremlin's power to threaten us. Some statements from even the highest officials of our government have suggested that the Soviet peoples, and especially the non-Russian nationalities within the Soviet Union, are ready to revolt and that "the entire rotten structure will collapse." Others have expressed the belief that the "relaxations" Khrushchev has ordered, including the reduction of police terror, have released forces—especially among intellectuals —which are undermining the Kremlin's authority. Some have reported dangerous discontent due to lack of consumer goods, while others maintain that the better life Khrushchev has promised is diverting attention from world conquest to domestic comfort. A few have seen in Khrushchev's reforms of the educational system signs of dangerous unrest among Soviet students, who are demanding more independence and freedom of expression.

Some economists and political analysts have suggested that Khrushchev's decentralization of industry is threatening the power of the central planners and creating frictions between national interests and parochial provincial interests. Khrushchev's efforts to solve the endemic food problem have not, it is sometimes reported, come up to expectations and are threatened by catastrophes such as giant dust bowls in the newly plowed "virgin lands." Some population experts have found evidence of serious labor shortages due to the sharp decline in the birth rate during the war years. On the other hand, many highly competent students of Soviet affairs have reported other findings and have come to conclusions quite the contrary of those above.

Even in a trip as extensive as the one I took it was obviously impossible to cover every aspect of Soviet affairs. I therefore concentrated on these specific key sectors, seeking answers to the vital questions which, I think, tend to confuse our thinking and muddle our policies toward the Kremlin.

I spent more than six weeks traveling some 18,000 miles within the Soviet Union by plane, train, boat and car (and a good deal on foot), visiting Central Russia and the Ukraine, the Volga area and Central Asia, the Kazakh steppes and the Ural industrial area. Finally I flew by Soviet jet three thousand miles into the heart of Siberia north of Lake Baikal to inspect one of the gigantic power projects the Soviets are carrying out in the taiga. Many cities and projects I visited had been closed to foreigners. Some had never before been seen by an American.

I spoke with hundreds of collective farmers and factory workers, municipal and provincial officials, scientists, professors, economists and planners. These detailed discussions culminated in lengthy talks in the Kremlin with leading government officials and finally in several talks with Mr. Khrushchev lasting many hours.

This volume tells what I found out about the changes which have taken place since Stalin's death, what new developments have occurred, what new attitudes have been created by Khrushchev's new approach to old Russian problems, and finally what conclusions I reached, especially as these changes affect our relations with the U.S.S.R.

CHAPTER TWO

Russia for the Russians?

THE SINGLE MOST VITAL question anyone examining Soviet policy must ask is: Do the Soviet leaders still consider their first objective world revolution and their primary task today to make the Soviet Union a bastion from which to launch their assault on the non-Communist world, or are they beginning to modify their global ambitions and bend their energies to building a Russia for the Russians in which the Soviet citizens can enjoy the high standard of living which their skills and resources entitle them to?

When I was in the Soviet Union as American Ambassador in 1946 much of the Soviet Union from its western frontiers to Stalingrad 1,500 miles to the east lay largely in ruins. Its fields were scorched and barren. Its villages had in many cases been burned to the ground. Those factories which had not been evacuated to the Urals had been destroyed. But now with their remarkable energy the Russian people were once more cultivating the wheat-bearing steppes; they had rebuilt the villages and reconstructed industry.

Since my departure I had followed the reports that Soviet economic strength had far surpassed the prewar levels and that the standard of living of the people was higher than it had been since the Revolution. The sputnik had demonstrated the genius of its scientists and the skill of its engineers. Perhaps, as some Americans had suggested, all these accomplishments had cooled the ardor of the Kremlin leaders for world revolution. Perhaps at last there was a tendency to develop the Russian economy for the benefit of the Russian people rather than to give first priority to building a powerful base for world Communism.

What I found in answer to the question was profoundly disturbing.

When I first visited the Soviet Union in 1926 a bitter conflict was raging over the future of the Soviet Union. Some, adhering strictly to the teachings of Karl Marx, had argued that Communist Russia could not survive unless the rest of the world went Communist. Stalin, on the other hand, contended that a Communist state could survive in a capitalist world and that the Soviet Union should devote all its energies to developing its industrial power as the bastion for the defense of Communism and as a base for world Communist domination.

In the years that followed Stalin had established his personal dictatorship and at appalling sacrifice to the Russian people had started the drive for industrialization. When Hitler struck, Stalin already had the beginnings of a powerful industrial and military base.

"If Hitler had given me just one more year," he told me when I first saw him in 1941, "we could have thrown back the invaders."

At the outset of hostilities, however, Stalin was well aware that to rally the patriotism of the Soviet people he must proclaim the conflict as the "Fatherland War." He told me that the Russian people had always bravely resisted every invader. "The only difference between the last world war and this one," he said to me, "is that the Czar gave them ax handles to fight with. We have given them rifles.

"We are under no illusions that they are fighting for us," he said, meaning the Communist Party. "They are fighting for Mother Russia."

He reversed the propaganda that had depicted the history of the country as beginning with the October Revolution of 1917. He extolled the heroes of Russian history—Kutusov, Suvorov, Peter the Great and Ivan. Before the German invasion a moving picture had been started on the life of Ivan the Terrible, portraying him in good Communist fashion as the cruel oppressor. But after the war had started, the producer, Sergei Eisenstein, told me he had received peremptory orders to scrap the film and to begin with a completely new approach. Ivan the Terrible, it was made clear to him, should be recast as Ivan the Great, the man who led and fought for the Russian people against the boyars, the feudal lords.

This switch was not difficult for Stalin, as he had a great sense of Russia's historic role. One of the friends I made in Moscow was the Soviet historical novelist Alexis Tolstoy, a former aristocrat and a distant relative of the great Russian novelist Leo Tolstoy who had accepted life under the Communist regime. We often discussed Russian history, and when he died late in the war I was asked to be an honorary pallbearer.

"If you want to understand the Kremlin of today," he once said, "you must first understand the Kremlin of Ivan and Peter."

He emphasized the historic isolation of Russia from the rest of the world and the fear, suspicion and dislike of foreigners that had always prevailed and that still deeply influenced the Kremlin. My many dealings with Stalin confirmed his analysis. To illustrate his point he recalled that it used to be said in pre-revolution rural Russia that a peasant would welcome a stranger and share his last loaf of bread and bottle of vodka and his roof with him, but on waking next morning he might suspect he had been fooled and would cut the stranger's throat and appropriate his money.

He also told the story, hardly reassuring to a frequent visitor to the Kremlin, of a foreign ambassador to the court of one of the early Czars who, misunderstanding the court ceremony, had appeared before the Czar with his hat on. "If you don't care to take your hat off in my presence," the Czar had shouted angrily, "you need never take it off again." Whereupon he ordered his soldiers to drive a spike through the unfortunate envoy's hat and skull.

At the end of the war Stalin had explained to me his plans to rebuild and develop the political and economic potential of the Soviet Union. He wanted to develop its power to the point that it would never again be at the mercy of an invader. His establishment of Communist regimes in Eastern Europe was designed not only to spread the faith but also to prevent anti-Soviet regimes from once more springing up on his western frontier.

"I will not tolerate a new *cordon sanitaire,*" he said repeatedly, meaning a belt of anti-Soviet states on the Soviet Union's western frontier as it existed before World War II.

Furthermore, he saw in the postwar dislocations of Western Europe favorable conditions for the spread of Communism—a possibility that might well have become a reality had it not been for the Truman Doctrine and the Marshall Plan.

I had the impression that Stalin regarded himself on a par

with Lenin as a co-author of the creed he called Marxism-Leninism-Stalinism, and that he never felt himself tied to any specific doctrine or dogma. If it interfered with his plans he found some way of changing it.

In my recent visit to the Soviet Union I had several prolonged talks with Khrushchev and had an opportunity to compare him with his predecessor Stalin. It seemed to me that whereas Stalin was a prophet of the Marxist creed, Khrushchev is basically a disciple and, like most disciples, even more fanatically faithful to its doctrines. Moreover, Khrushchev now has several rival high priests of Communism—Mao Tse-tung in China, Tito in Yugoslavia and, to a lesser degree, Gomulka in Poland.

In many other respects as well the two men are quite different. Stalin was small and had a withered arm. His complexion was sallow and pockmarked. I always had the feeling he was handicapped by his appearance. Whenever he posed for a picture with others he made a point of sitting forward so that the foreshortening made him look bigger. Yet he was a man of great dignity, with a withdrawn, reserved manner. He seldom joked and was sparing of words.

Khrushchev too is short, though stout. But he seems to have no concern about his appearance, and his suits hang loosely on his round frame. He moves constantly and every gesture is dynamic. There is nothing reserved about Khrushchev. "I don't like to read," he admitted to a congress of writers when I was in Moscow. "I like to talk."

Khrushchev also likes to boast, to bluff and to threaten. Often he loses his temper and his face flushes as he wags his finger under your chin. But a moment later he is calm again and proposes a toast to friendship. He is a consummate actor and obviously enjoys making an impression on his audience. In some respects he may be more dangerous than

Stalin, because he is less calculating and careful and more impulsive. But he is certainly less ruthless and arbitrary. It has been suggested he is like Hitler, but I found no resemblance whatever. Khrushchev though tough and determined, though a fanatical Communist and a devout believer in Marxist doctrine, is intensely human, gregarious and even boisterous.

There is of course a continuous process of interpreting the Marxist dogma, and Khrushchev indulges in this himself. As he explained it to me, "We make it more precise." For example, at our first meeting when we were discussing the possibility of another war he told me almost with surprise that "American ideologists refuse to understand the current Soviet doctrine on the likelihood of war." Wars between capitalists and Communists were, he thought, unlikely unless the West started one, which he said would be ill-advised since in five to seven years the Soviets would be stronger than the West. Marx, he went on, had taught that "imperialist wars" between capitalist countries were inevitable and that during them the "workers" would use the arms the capitalists had given them to fight the enemy, in order to overthrow their capitalist regimes. This interpretation, Khrushchev said, had been "made more precise" by the Twentieth Communist Party Congress, which had decreed that imperialist wars in future would still be possible but not inevitable. To clinch the argument he added that this new definition had been confirmed by the Twenty-first Communist Party Congress. In other words, I gather that not only he but we Americans as well should accept the authority of a Communist Party congress to predetermine the future course of our own history.

Unlike the skeptical ex-theologian Stalin, Khrushchev the peasant devoutly believes in the Marxist gospel. Communism, he told me with deep conviction, is a higher form of social, political and economic organization. By the Marxist "law of historic inevitability" it is bound to replace capitalism throughout the world.

Nevertheless, he has not hesitated to repudiate Stalin and to change his methods wherever they caused discontent and resistance, slowing down production in the factory and the farm. Khrushchev has immense pride in the great industrial progress the Soviet Union has made since the war and in the improvement in living standards of the people, both of which he believes will help promote world Communism.

Stalin had said that Communism would take root where the conditions of the workers under capitalism became intolerable. Khrushchev, on the other hand, predicted that one day the workers in the rest of the world would be persuaded by the superiority of Soviet conditions to adopt the Communist system. Sooner or later, he kept repeating, capitalism would be overthrown.

As though to reassure me, he added that the timing of these uprisings would depend on the conditions in each individual country and would be determined not by the Kremlin but by the workers in each country. However, he made it abundantly clear that when the time was decided, the Soviet Union would render all necessary assistance to assure the success of the revolution.

Turning to the United States, Khrushchev told me that a Communist revolution was still far off but we too were inevitably approaching the fateful event. Already, he maintained, the rate of national growth in America was reaching the stagnation point and eventually the stagnation would lead to unemployment. The workers would sink in misery and finally rise up and join the world revolution.

Again and again he referred to the class struggle in the

United States, and when I denied there was such a thing he answered, "The class struggle is an international matter"— indicating that no nation could by domestic action avoid its consequences in the long run.

"Thus far," he went on as we sat talking in the Kremlin, "your great natural resources and the enormous profits you accumulated in both world wars have enabled the capitalist rulers of America to buy off or bribe the working class with high wages and high living standards."

I retorted that the United States had made no profits during the wars. Perhaps, I told him, he confused increased production in war years with profit making. In that case, I added, the Soviet war plants behind the Ural Mountains which had made most of Russia's tanks and artillery had also made great profits for the Soviet government. The United States, I further reminded him, had given the Soviet Union no less than eleven billion dollars in aid during the war. Hastily Khrushchev acknowledged the gift and expressed his country's deep appreciation and thankfulness for the valuable assistance it had received during the war from the United States.

Nevertheless, he went on, the United States is ruled by a small clique of businessmen and financiers who are making their fortunes by selling arms to the American government. It is this small "clique," he told me with apparent conviction, who actually rule the United States and keep the cold war alive.

"The workers have no say in your government," he went on. They are, he indicated, merely the slaves of capitalism. When I retorted by reminding him of the frequency of free elections in America and their total absence in the Communist orbit, he answered angrily, "Your ideas and mine on the subject of slavery, freedom and free elections will never coincide." Then to drive home his point he added, "Do you suppose we consider it a free election when the voters of New York State have a choice only between a Harriman and a Rockefeller?"

Time and again Khrushchev repeated the argument that a small group of businessmen were encouraging the cold war in order to make profits for themselves and that without arms production the American economy would decline and vast unemployment would be inevitable. The idea advanced by some on our side of the Atlantic that the Kremlin is spurring on the arms race in order to force Americans to spend themselves into bankruptcy is hard to reconcile with this standard tenet of Communist doctrine to which Khrushchev so firmly adheres.

Returning to the subject of the American "workers," I suggested to Khrushchev that he come to the United States someday and talk to American workers and visit their homes. They might have something to teach him.

But Khrushchev dismissed the idea as useless. "We have nothing to learn from American workers," he said.

I suggested too that he talk with American labor leaders. "You are a coal miner by profession. Come over and meet some of our important union leaders."

"They are mere lackeys of the ruling class," Khrushchev replied, repeating the time-worn Marxist formulas. "We want to talk to men of decision—capitalists like yourself," he added with a patronizing pat on my arm. "You are the people who decide in the United States."

Furthermore, he continued, he knew the workers of America far better than a capitalist like myself ever could. "I was a humble worker myself," he said. "I started life as a shepherd, was promoted to a cowherd and eventually got a job in the mines, where I stayed till the Revolution."

As though not to be outdone, Deputy Premier Anastas Mikoyan, who with Deputy Premier Frol Kozlov and Foreign Minister Andrei Gromyko had joined the discussion, broke in: "And I was the son of a shoemaker." Kozlov said, "And I was a homeless waif." Even Gromyko, who had sat in glum silence throughout the conversation, spoke up: "And I was the son of a pauper."

I told them they all sounded like American politicians on the stump boasting of their log-cabin origins, but they were not convinced. As Communists they had been taught by the works of Karl Marx exactly how the world would develop and there was little hope of showing them how false their concepts were.

These talks with Khrushchev and other high officials of the Soviet government and the Communist Party were enough to disabuse me of any lingering ideas that perhaps the Soviet leaders of today are relaxing their efforts to replace the free governments of the world with "dictatorships of the proletariat" modeled on the Kremlin. Their plans for developing a Russia for the Russians are subordinate to the main goal of world revolution. Though their methods have changed since Stalin's time, their aim remains the same.

However, the Communist Party contains in its ranks only eight million of the two hundred and ten million Soviet citizens, and I suspect that not even all of these are as fanatical or true-believing as the men presently in the Kremlin.

Among nonparty Russians, particularly in the younger generation, I found much evidence—confirmed by other foreign observers in Moscow—that their dominant desire is to improve their own living conditions, and that they have little interest in the furtherance of Communist ambitions abroad. The engineer, the Army officer or the teacher, I suspect, is more interested in getting an apartment for himself, then a small refrigerator for his wife, or even on some distant day a little car for his family, than he is in bringing the "blessings of Communism" to the peoples of Africa or Indonesia. Their acceptance of the necessity for a strong military establishment is based on the belief pounded into them by Kremlin propagandists that American warmongers may start another war and once again destroy the gains they have made in the last decade. Everywhere I went I found that the preservation of peace was uppermost in their minds.

Furthermore, as I traveled throughout the provinces from the Baltic to the Himalayas, I found Soviet officials who seemed considerably less concerned with the "class struggle" in Detroit than with the development of the local resources of the Ukraine or Tadzhikistan. It seemed to me their absorbing interest was the development of their local economy and the satisfaction of their own needs.

Perhaps one day these influences will play a role in the councils of the Kremlin. But at the present time I find no evidence that the cause of world revolution lies any more lightly than before upon the leaders in the Kremlin who now rule the Soviet Union's destiny.

CHAPTER THREE

The Powder Keg Myth

THE SOVIET PEOPLE, Americans are sometimes told even by persons in high office, are in a state of incipient revolt. The Communist leaders in the Kremlin, it is said, are sitting on a powder keg. If the West gives them encouragement the Soviet people are ready to rise and overthrow the Communist regime. This was one of the ideas I wanted to explore in the Soviet Union. I found no evidence to justify any such theory.

During my 18,000-mile journey around the country I talked to hundreds of people in all walks of life. While I found gripes and dissatisfaction with some aspects of life, I found no evidence of any organized opposition. These conclusions were confirmed by all the foreign observers I talked with in the Soviet Union. The great mass of the Soviet people have, I believe, accepted the Communist regime, or at least have acquiesced in it, and entertain no ideas of overthrowing it.

In 1926 when I went to Russia many people were still predicting that within a few years the Communist regime would collapse. At that time many adherents of the Czarist cause and many followers of Kerensky were still at liberty —some of them kept on at their old jobs as technicians in key posts, even in the Army, until the Bolsheviks could train substitutes for them. Many too believed that eventually they could organize a counterrevolution and throw the Communists out of the Kremlin. But the Bolsheviks had been rounding up the more troublesome dissidents and sending them to exile in Siberia or even shooting them.

Eventually Stalin liquidated not only the old Czarist elements and counterrevolutionists but also many old Bolsheviks within the party who had opposed his ruthless rule. After one of his close lieutenants, Sergei Kirov, was asassinated in Leningrad in 1934, he began the awful purges that lasted almost up to the outbreak of war in 1941. By then any hopes of overthrowing Stalin's regime were stifled.

In that period he was busy building his industrial base and demanding incredible sacrifices of his subjects. During my recent visit one of Khrushchev's close associates said to me, "In those days Stalin spared neither himself nor anyone else. But," he added, "the period of want and poverty is gone."

Khrushchev, he went on to say, is a new man in a new era, and the Soviet Union need no longer suffer for every factory, mine and collective farm organized.

While to America the way Russians live would be considered one of hardship, to the Russians themselves when they look back on the terrible twenties and thirties it is a life of real progress.

In Stalin's day everything they did was for the future. *Budyet*—It will be—was the theme of Stalinist propapanda and of the hundreds of anti-Stalinist jokes that circulated among the population. Today the Russians believe that the doubtful promises of Stalin are beginning to come true. "It will be" has, they think, become "it is."

Furthermore, they regard their progress as great national accomplishments of which they are intensely proud. Though many of their boasts, and especially those of Mr. Khrushchev himself, are wildly extravagant, they can perhaps be better understood if one appreciates the immense sufferings they have gone through to reach the level of existence they enjoy today.

Just as Stalin induced the Russians to fight courageously for Mother Russia, Khrushchev has, it seems to me, induced them to work hard for the expansion of their economy in peacetime as a patriotic duty. When I was inspecting one of the great new hydroelectric plants on the Volga at Stalingrad a couple of young workers came up to me. "Have you a dam as large as this one?" they asked eagerly. When I told them about Grand Coulee and they learned it was just about the same size, their faces fell a little. But then one of them said, "You should see the dam at Bratsk. It's much bigger than this." I told them I was going to Siberia to see the Bratsk dam, which I understood would in fact have twice the capacity of Grand Coulee. They were greatly pleased.

If Khrushchev one day is thrown out or a struggle for power arises among his successors, it will not, I believe, be as a result of basic dissatisfaction on the part of the Soviet population. Nor is it likely to result in a radical rejection of the "socialist" system, as he called it, in favor of a genuine democracy.

Closely associated with the myth of incipient revolt against the Communist regime is the belief still entertained by many people in America that the Soviet national minorities, the Ukrainians, the White Russians, the Uzbeks or the

Tadzhiks, seething with unrest, are about to rise up against the Russian yoke. During my travels I visited five of the so-called republics constituting the Soviet Union. While the historic resentment against Moscow rule continues, I find little support for the theory that active resistance might flare up at any time. On the contrary, I found a new challenge to America's leadership among backward countries throughout the world.

During the war I had discussed with Stalin the problems posed by the non-Russian nationalities within the Soviet Union, which comprise almost half the entire population, speaking upwards of eighty-seven different languages. This problem was one of Stalin's special interests and the first task to which he was assigned by Lenin after the October Revolution in 1917, when he was appointed Commissar for Nationalities. Stalin's answer to the problem differed from the old Czarist policy of Russification in two ways. First, Stalin tried to sugar-coat the sovietization of these areas with carefully controlled self-expression in a limited field of national culture and folklore. In the second place, he made a determined effort to raise the productivity and living standards of these backward peoples in order to increase their contribution to the industrialization of the Soviet Union as a whole.

The sugar-coating of sovietization did not always work. Deeply suspicious of the rise of nationalism in these areas, Stalin—particularly during the thirties and again during the war—employed the most brutal methods to break up any potential nuclei of separatism and frequently curtailed even the limited rights of the minorities to cultural autonomy.

One minority in particular, the Jews, he treated with great cruelty. He exiled tens of thousands to the artificially created Jewish republic of Birobidjan in the Far East. In addition he suppressed their religion, their writers and their theaters and eventually eliminated all Jews but Lazar Kaganovich from the top posts in the regime. One by one Kamenev, Zinoviev, Radek and many others were dismissed from their important posts and exiled, imprisoned or shot.

Even under Khrushchev the position of the Jews has been a difficult one, and although I met some Jews in important technical jobs I did not find a single Jew in a high political position. When Mikoyan was in New York, Senator Herbert Lehman had tried to intercede with him on behalf of the Jews, and I heard a report that as a result of his efforts a Jewish newspaper had been re-established in Kiev. But when I got to Kiev and asked whether a paper was being published, I was told very bluntly that none was.

In the larger cities we visited I was told by officials that Orthodox and Baptist churches and a few synagogues were functioning. My wife and I and members of my party attended several church services. The churches were well attended, and generally the worshipers seemed as well dressed as the average people on the street. We saw some poverty-stricken old people in the churches but also men and women whose clothing indicated they came from the higher-income groups. Young people as well as old attended the services.

In Tashkent the Moslem mufti was absent but I called on his assistant, an unimpressive but outspoken propagandist for the Soviet regime. I also visited Tashkent's principal mosque and its religious library, which in addition to numerous ancient commentaries on the Koran included an extensive file of *Pravda*.

On the material side, there is no doubt that the national minorities of the Soviet Union have vastly improved their conditions under Soviet rule. Perhaps the most striking and symbolic example of this improvement I saw in one of the smallest and most remote of the republics, Tadzhikistan, deep in Central Asia on the Chinese and Afghan frontiers (its capital, Stalinabad, is in fact a thousand miles closer to New Delhi than to Moscow).

During the early years of the Revolution, Tadzhikistan was a hotbed of counterrevolution. In the Pamir Mountains, a spur of the Himalayas in eastern Tadzhikistan, the famous adventurer Enver Pasha made his last stand against Soviet troops in the late twenties. Not until 1929 was the area sufficiently subdued to permit the establishment of an "autonomous Soviet republic" and for many years it was a forbidden area strictly closed to all foreigners. In fact, few foreigners have been admitted even in recent years.

Perhaps this explained the complaint with which I was greeted when I called on the Tadzhik Prime Minister, Mr. Dodokhudoev. "Americans," he said, "have never even heard of our republic."

He told me that the population of Tadzhikistan is about two million and that since the Revolution it has developed a flourishing economy based on the production of high-grade cotton and textiles.

When the republic was founded thirty years ago and Stalinabad selected as its capital, the latter was a typical Central Asian village of only a few thousand inhabitants living chiefly in mud huts without sanitation, water, hospitals, or even schools. After Stalin's troops had smashed the power of the feudal landlords and rulers and their archaic practices and customs, the Soviet government had invested heavily in the area not only to stimulate the local economy but also to develop its educational, health and agricultural systems.

Today Stalinabad is a bustling town of two hundred thousand inhabitants and the republic itself boasts a rapidly expanding industrial and agricultural economy. The low-yield short-staple cotton which formerly produced only a few thousand tons yearly has been replaced by long-staple varieties with yields which, Tadzhik officials claim, compare favorably with those of California and last year produced for the republic an income of over two hundred million dollars. In addition, new dams and irrigation canals were designed with the help of three American engineers to provide almost a million acres of new cultivated land. A textile mill was built in Stalinabad which today turns out over fifty million yards of fabric for the Soviet market.

Besides the textile plant, Tadzhikistan has a number of food-processing plants, a silk factory and a plant to manufacture cotton gins. It boasts thirty-six electric power plants, and in recent years large deposits of petroleum as well as of coal, zinc and lead have been discovered.

Aside from the normal difficulties of developing a modern economy from the primitive base of a Central Asian feudal community, the builders of modern Tadzhikistan have had to cope with many other handicaps. No railroad reached Stalinabad until the Soviets built one after the Revolution. The rapid expansion of the irrigation system has caused serious loss of fertility through salinization of the soil. Thousands of illiterate peasants had to be trained to operate not only the agricultural machinery of the cotton farms but the looms and spindles of the textile plant.

In addition to raising the industrial and agricultural level of the economy, the Soviet authorities have made great efforts to improve both health and education.

Thirty years ago, I was told, there was scarcely a doctor in all of Tadzhikistan. Today there are over two thousand, one for each 870 inhabitants (as against about one to 700 in the U.S.), and for every 240 there is one trained nurse.

Stalinabad has a number of new hospitals, including two
children's hospitals; I visited one of these with my wife and
found it reasonably well equipped and its personnel competent.

Malaria and trachoma, which have ravaged the population of Central Asia for centuries, were until recently endemic in Tadzhikistan. "Anyone who had not had malaria
hadn't lived," an official told me. But today, he explained,
swamp drainage and the mass use of insecticides has practically eliminated malaria to the point that doctors are complaining they do not have enough cases for research purposes. Trachoma has likewise been reduced, by the use of
antibiotics. During our stay in Tadzhikistan no one in my
party saw a case of blindness or infected eyes, those telltale
symptoms of trachoma which one notices in bazaars in
other countries of Asia.

In the newer sections of Stalinabad one finds imposing
government buildings and three- and four-story apartment
buildings, some of them gaily painted and decorated with
delicate filigree work copied from ancient Persian models.
Other sections have been reserved for individual private
housing—small bungalows with tidy gardens. In the older
sections of town one still sees the thatched mud huts and
the narrow unpaved alleys where running water is rare and
sewage practically nonexistent, but the filth and the flies one
usually associates with Central Asian adobe towns have
been practically eliminated. In nearby Samarkand an official explained why: "We have to keep our towns clean. In
our semitropical climate filth spells disease." And disease,
every Soviet official has been taught, is the bane of productivity.

The Soviet authorities have also made a major drive in
the field of education which has converted Tadzhikistan

from a country of illiterates into an educated community. In 1929 scarcely 150 pupils attended Tadzhikistan's three schools. Already the system has produced 50,000 specialists with higher or technical education, and 330,000 students are enrolled in its 2,600 schools.

In addition to the schools, the Prime Minister of Tadzhikistan boasted, they now have over a thousand of the ever present Soviet "palaces of culture" where people can go in the evenings to listen to lectures and watch performances of visiting troupes of actors, musicians and entertainers, or to participate in amateur theatricals and music. The republic boasts 800 libraries, 450 movies and over 500 newspapers, to say nothing of the many "parks of culture and rest."

At the Stalinabad Library, I was shown with pride some ancient illuminated Persian manuscripts, as well as twenty-nine technical journals from the United States. In addition to the usual translations of Theodore Dreiser, Jack London and Sinclair Lewis, the head librarian told me the most popular American book was the *The Gadfly,* by Ethel Lilian Voynich, an English immigrant, written at the end of the last century. Though most Americans have long since forgotten this somewhat radical novel, the librarian assured me it was one of the greatest American classics and among the most widely read books in our country.

Tadzhikistan also has seven institutes of higher learning, including a university and three teachers' colleges, with a total enrollment of over thirty thousand students. In these institutions specialists are being trained not only in agriculture, medicine and science but also in historical research and archaeology.

But perhaps Tadzhikistan's proudest boast is its Academy of Sciences. Its president, Professor S. U. Umarov, told me that it operates thirteen separate research institutes in the fields of geology, chemistry, biology, agriculture, as well as in the humanities. These institutes are investigating practically every aspect of Tadzhikistan's natural resources, soil conditions, flora and fauna, ancient and modern history and culture, and even its rich prehistoric anthropological past.

In a later chapter I shall return to the academies of sciences which I visited in the capitals of Central Asia and in other Soviet cities, and which play so important a part in the Soviet research and scientific system. Here I would like to stress their role in the nationalities problem which has faced every ruler of Russia and the Soviet Union.

The colonial system of the Czarist regime was designed primarily to force upon the natives a Russian administration under a Russian governor and to attempt to assimilate them by requiring those who wanted to rise above the lowest status of workers to learn the Russian language. In other respects the Czarist regime had hardly begun to raise the primitive economic level of the area.

Stalin's system also imposed a Soviet administration by representatives appointed from Moscow. While Russian is still required of native officials and indeed by all who attended schools, most instruction is today given in the native language, and in other aspects of the national culture the native races are given at least the appearance of autonomy. Politically, neither under the Czars nor under the Soviets has there been any real autonomy.

When I visited Tashkent in 1944, the Prime Minister was a genial native Uzbek but I gained the impression that the real power was wielded by his deputy, a dour Russian who was obviously a Communist Party agent. While visiting the Central Exhibition grounds in Moscow in 1959 I found the former Prime Minister in charge of the Uzbek pavilion, a demotion which, it seemed to me, confirmed my earlier impression.

Just before my recent visit to Central Asia, two of the three highest officials of Uzbekistan were dismissed by Moscow without any explanation and replaced by others appointed by the central Soviet authorities. This shows the tight rein with which Moscow still governs. On the other hand, by its heavy investments in industry, agriculture, education and public health the Soviet regime has contributed to a substantial rise in the native standard of living and intellectual growth—as the local academies of sciences demonstrate. While these investments were made chiefly to increase the area's contribution to the total Soviet economy, the end effect has been to provide material and intellectual benefits to the native populations and to create a genuine pride in their achievements. This, I suspect, has mitigated the absence of real political freedom or power of self-determination.

I believe too that in some areas I did not visit and in some circles I did not come into contact with there is both resentment and a suppressed desire for local political autonomy. Even among native officials I detected a self-conscious awareness of their political dependency. The mayor of one town, for example, while entertaining me for dinner made a long speech about the ability of Asians—of whom he considered himself one—to assimilate conquerors.

"You Westerners," he said, "have made much of the subjugation of India by the Moguls—who, incidentally, were Uzbeks. The fact is, however, that the Indians assimilated the invaders within three generations." The parallel to the Soviet position in Central Asia was too obvious to miss and I began to wonder how he was going to escape charges of treason. But then he added with a smile, "Of course, the situation does not arise here, because we and the Soviet Russians have joined in a voluntary federation from which we derive mutual benefits."

The "mutual benefits" which I saw in Stalinabad were also apparent in the other republics I visited. The position of the native officials, however, varied from area to area. In Uzbekistan and Tadzhikistan the great majority of officials I met were Central Asians. In Kazakhstan, farther north, although the Prime Minister of the republic and the mayor of its capital, Alma-Ata, and one or two senior officials were native Kazakhs, the heads of the all-important economic councils and the principle industrial plants were exclusively Russians. In one Kazakh town where I was entertained at a banquet of thirty or forty officials I asked how many present were Kazakhs. Two responded—one a news photographer and the other a minor functionary.

I also found that in Kazakhstan the Russians made little effort to hide their superior position. If a Kazakh official wanted to propose a toast, for example, when he asked the senior Russian official for permission occasionally he was peremptorily told to sit down.

There are, I believe, two reasons for this difference. In the first place, the Kazakhs, as they are the first to admit, have never had a national culture or tradition. Until Stalin collectivized them in the late twenties the great majority were nomads wandering about the arid steppe grazing their huge flocks of sheep. The Prime Minister, Mr. D. A. Kunaev, a tall handsome Kazakh, told me with pride that he had been born in one of the big black nomad tents on the shores of Lake Balkash, where his father grazed his flocks. A senior official of the Kazakh Academy of Sciences said that until thirty years ago he was still an illiterate nomad.

In the second place, the natural resources of Kazakhstan, far more than in any other Central Asian republic, have been exploited and their production has been integrated into the Soviet national economy. In recent years huge iron and coal mines have been opened far beyond the needs of the republic or its capacity to develop them. Much of the "virgin-lands" area which Khrushchev has plowed up is located within Kazakhstan. The technical and scientific skills to open the mines, build the steel mills and manage the huge state farms are beyond the capabilities of most Kazakhs.

But despite their obviously inferior position, I detected no outward friction between them and their Soviet exploiters.

"We had no national culture of our own," one of them told me. "What we have now has been borrowed from the Russians. Kazakhstan without the Russians would be a fish without water."

That the Soviet authorities have been able to dominate the nationalities of Central Asia without visible signs of friction and to rule them with a complete absence of free democratic institutions or rights of self-determination is also perhaps due to the fact that these groups have never known such institutions. Before their subjugation by the Russians they had been ruled througout history by tyrannical potentates and their numbers decimated in periodic fratricidal wars. In fact, even the highly developed nationalities of European Russia have not known independence for generations. Only in the reconquered Baltic States and the former territories of Poland and Czechoslovakia and Rumania have the populations known anything for centuries but Czarist or Soviet authoritarianism.

Since my trip was confined to the Soviet Union, this volume does not deal with the problems of the satellites of

Eastern Europe. Nor did I travel in the newly acquired territories of western Russia and the Baltic. I have not, therefore, expressed any judgments on these areas.

When I was traveling in the traditionally Russian areas of the Soviet Union or in the territories colonialized by the Czars, I found little evidence that the populations are seething with discontent or that the Communist leaders in the Kremlin are sitting on a powder keg. There is doubtless dissatisfaction among the Soviet population with many aspects of daily life. Among the non-Russians in particular there remain indications of the traditional repugnance for Great Russian domination. But the dissatisfactions, so far as I could see in Central Asia, were not of the magnitude to provoke uprisings, and the minorities' resentment at Russian rule has to a considerable extent been mitigated by the great material advances they have won under the Soviet regime.

The most disturbing aspect of this rapid economic development from a poor peasant community in the brief space of one generation is the effect it may have on the people of other underdeveloped areas. Every year thousands of visitors from Southeast Asia pour through the big international airport of Tashkent and are taken on tours of the gigantic model collective farms, malaria-free villages, and big factories producing everything from shoes to heavy agricultural machinery, to say nothing of the schools, universities, hospitals and opera houses. These developments provide telling ammunition to the Communist parties of Southeast Asia, who point them out to those who are impatient to develop their countries. To peoples with little understanding of the values of free institutions they provide a tempting alternative to the slower procedures of democracy.

As such they are an important part of the challenge Mr.

Khrushchev is making to the Western democracies, and particularly the United States, of competition for world leadership. If we are to meet that challenge we must, I believe, show a greater understanding of the problems and aspirations of those seeking to improve their status, and we must make greater efforts to help them achieve those aims rapidly—and in freedom. For in addition to providing material aid, we must also by example and encouragement provide assistance in strengthening their democratic political and social institutions while they strive to build modern industrial economics.

CHAPTER FOUR

The Consumer Comes Last

EVER SINCE I LEFT the Soviet Union in 1946, and particularly since Khrushchev came to power, there have been reliable reports of a slow but steady rise in the Soviet standard of living from the miserable sub-subsistence level it reached during the war years. These reports have given rise to a theory that as their essential demands for a tolerable living are met the Soviet people will demand more and more and insist that they be given a greater share of national production in the form of consumer goods.

Stalin once said to me, referring to Hitler's gobbling up of Europe, that a man's appetite grows with eating. Will the Soviet people's appetite grow to the point of forcing the Kremlin to give in to their demands?

My findings on this subject have been mixed. Certainly the Soviet living standard is very low compared to our own. It has made rapid progress in the past few years. Appetites too are growing. Khrushchev is, I believe, finding it more difficult to satisfy these appetites and at the same time devote over half the total national production to investments and armaments. However, I saw little evidence that these demands are so pressing that in the foreseeable future he will be forced to cut his investments either in heavy industry or in armaments below the minimum he believes necessary to achieve Soviet aims.

My wife and I were particularly interested in finding out just how badly or how well the average Soviet citizen is faring at present—and especially the women, who, I was told, outnumber the men by ten million as a result of war casualties.

The first thing that strikes every visitor to the Soviet Union is how many women have jobs. I was never able to get an accurate figure on exactly what proportion of women were employed, but one official estimated it at around ninety per cent of those under sixty. The main reason is that to bring up a family today one salary is not enough, so the mother as well as the father—and often the children—must contribute to the family budget.

But even in families where this is not necessary, among higher-paid engineers or officials, I found the women working. In Bratsk in the heart of Siberia, the construction chief's wife was a teacher of botany. Deputy Premier Frol Kozlov told me, "My wife can't bear sitting at home doing nothing." (Mrs. Kozlov has a job as an engineer in a scientific research institute.) One of the few "unemployed" housewives I heard of was Mrs. Nikita Khrushchev—and I daresay her official duties leave little time for just "sitting at home doing nothing."

Many women have gone into engineering and research work, but the chief occupations among educated women, I found, are medicine, teaching and language study. Every doctor I met in my travels was a woman.

The Soviets were among the first to preach the equality of women, but I found they had not yet applied this principle to the official government hierarchy. Some of the heads of local health and education departments were women but all the mayors I met were men. In the universities and the academies of sciences I visited, scarcely a single woman was among the leading professors and scientists. Except for Mme. Ekaterina Furtseva, member of the Soviet Presidium, there are no women in senior political posts.

On the other hand, much of the heavy work—particularly road building, driving steam rollers, operating scrapers, spreading tar and shoveling snow—has been reserved chiefly for women. On the collective farms I inspected, the majority of workers were invariably women. Not a single collective-farm chairman or state farm director was a woman, but I found women in charge of the cow barns of all the farms I visited. In many of the factories I visited I was told that the women were used only for light work but in the shops I saw many young girls operating heavy machine tools. In the management section the only women I saw were secretaries and stenographers.

Just what sort of life do these women and their families lead? I visited a number of their homes and my wife and I had many conversations with women workers all over the Soviet Union. From them I learned that the average family occupies a single room in a multiroom apartment. If there are children and its income is a bit above the average, the family may have an extra little room for the children. The mother and the women in the other two or three rooms of the apartment share the kitchen, or perhaps she cooks on an electric hot plate in her room. (The official rules for communal living specifically forbid occupants from draining hot water from radiators to make tea!)

Unlike our municipalities, the Soviet authorities have had no difficulty in staggering the opening hours of various offices and enterprises in order to relieve the strain on transportation. As a result, the chances are the wife goes to work and returns home at different hours than her husband. If she works on a shift in a factory she and her husband may even work at entirely different hours at least part of each month.

After she has gotten herself and her small children up, she feeds them breakfast—perhaps bread and butter and some grits or oatmeal (cold breakfast foods are still a luxury). Unless she has her elderly mother or mother-in-law living with her—which, though, it increases the crowding, is often a great convenience and is very widely resorted to—she must take her small children to a state nursery. These nurseries are often well run and clean and the children are well taken care of, though occasionally one reads in the Soviet press complaints of lax administration and unsanitary, crowded conditions.

She then goes on to her job, which, if she is lucky, is close by. In the past two years factories have been required to use a considerable portion of their profits to build housing for their workers in the neighborhood of the plant. Otherwise in the larger cities the women can take a subway or else squeeze into streetcars or buses. In that case it often takes from thirty to sixty minutes to get to work.

Every shift is eight hours except in heavy industrial jobs, where it has recently been reduced to seven and to only six on Saturdays. The factory usually has a canteen where the woman can get a hot lunch.

When work is over she collects her children and does her shopping. Since very few Soviet families enjoy the luxury of even a small refrigerator, she must buy such perishables as she needs daily. Whatever other items she may need— darning cotton, an electric-light bulb, stockings—she must generally also buy at this time. If these items are in short supply, as shoes are at present, she may have to stand in line for several hours, so these items she puts off buying until Sunday, when the shops remain open for just such customers.

Cooking the evening meal is another problem. Since several cooks working over the single stove in the apartment are apt to get into each other's way, the government rules for communal living often posted in the apartment strictly prescribe how they must behave in order to avoid friction.

As Mr. Khrushchev was quick to recognize when he came to power, the average Soviet diet was very limited. Even today a Soviet family has such meat as it can afford chiefly in a soup such as borsch, or in sausage. Fish is cheaper and easier to come by, either fresh, dried or canned, and is a major source of proteins. The Soviet Union imports large quantities of fish from Iceland, England and Scandinavia. Potatoes and cabbage are plentiful all the year round. Fresh vegetables in season can be bought at the town market place. In recent years fruits have become much more available, though they may be expensive.

The culinary art in the Soviet Union is not highly developed. A few years ago, to meet this deficiency, an elaborate cookbook was published, with colored plates in addition to recipes—many of them on how to combine canned or preserved foods.

After dinner, if the wife is not too exhausted and there is someone to look after the children, she and her husband may occasionally go to the theater or the movies. (Theaters and the opera are relatively cheap and the performances often excellent.) Otherwise the family crowds together in one small room with perhaps a radio or even a television set.

Why is this a tolerable life for a Soviet woman? The answer is, I am sure, that bad as they are, living conditions are on the way up. Some years ago a worker would advertise for a "corner" rather than a room, and the only food that was plentiful was coarse black bread.

During the war, among the items Stalin asked that we supply from America were boots and cloth for his soldiers. The civilians had to get along with what they had.

At the war's end, the problem was to get enough clothing to keep warm during the frigid winters. In the villages straw shoes or patched rubber boots were the best footwear available. Quilted coats were standard attire for men and women in Moscow itself.

But now at last the vague promises Stalin used to make are gradually becoming a reality under Khrushchev. Today conditions are substantially better than at any time since the Revolution. They are better than last year, better than yesterday—to the Western foreigner perhaps still very low but to the Soviet citizen a vast improvement.

Compared to five years ago, the shop windows are almost cornucopias of plenty. Where the women were satisfied with rubber shoes before, now there are high-heeled models available if you stand in line long enough. Instead of drab black coats the textile industry is turning out gaily printed fabrics and bright tweeds. Besides, there are even imported goods to be had—not just in Moscow but in the provinces as well. In Stalinabad I saw German-made Mechano sets for children on sale. In Stalingrad they were selling men's shoes made in Czechoslovakia. In a small waterside café in Yalta we found genuine Pilsner beer from Pilsen.

Khrushchev himself has complained about the unattractive clothing people are wearing, and even in provincial towns I saw dress stores called "fashion studios" where women in the upper-income brackets can have dresses made for them according to the lastest fashion available from abroad—often some years old.

In the bigger towns there are gift shops and camera shops where the latest Soviet imitations of Leicas are available. (In Germany, I am told, the camera manufacturers are seriously disturbed by the high quality and relatively low cost of Soviet cameras.) Toward the end of my trip I visited a Pioneer camp for young boys and girls deep in Siberia. To reach it from Moscow I had to fly eight hours in a jet, two more in a propeller plane and finally an hour in a speedboat. A number of the boys and girls in the camp had cameras with which they eagerly took pictures of the foreign visitors, while we just as eagerly photographed them with a Polaroid camera, which caused a near-riot when we gave them the quickly made pictures.

At the suggestion of Deputy Premier Frol Kozlov I visited a community cafeteria in one of the new apartment house developments on the outskirts of Moscow where not only were ready-cooked meals available but housewives back from work could buy semiprepared dishes that required only heating at home. I noticed breaded cutlets, stuffed fish, hot soups and stuffed tomatoes for sale at ten per cent less than the cafeteria price. When I told Kozlov about our Automats and cafeterias in America he replied, "Wonderful! Here we see capitalism and Communism following the same road to improve the welfare of their people." It was a highly unorthodox comment from the Marxist point of view, and when Kozlov subsequently visited the United States I daresay he found that American catering methods were pretty far ahead down the road.

Despite these improvements, the Soviet consumer industries are still strictly subordinated to heavy industry, which gets the lion's share of all capital investment.

The garment industry, for example, does not begin to meet the demand for dresses. Only the lucky few can find the right model and the right size on the rack when they go shopping on Sundays. Others must buy the material and make up their own dresses—or get their grandmothers to do it for them. One rarely passes a shoe store open for business outside of which there is not a line of women waiting to see if by chance it has the right model in their particular size.

Recently Khrushchev has been promising the Soviet population that in time they will catch up with and pass the American standard of living. But as I said to him, in this race his horses have not even come out onto the track. With a population of 210 million compared to our own 175 million, the Soviet gross national product is estimated to be only forty-five per cent of ours. But it is increasing at a far faster rate. This is the basis for Khrushchev's claim that the Soviet Union will in time catch up to us in per capita production.

Much has been made in the American press about the exorbitant prices the Soviet purchaser must pay for the ordinary essentials of life. Compared to salaries they are indeed extremely high. One reason for it is the extraordinarily high markup Soviet industry puts on consumer goods. In a Central Asian textile plant I saw a bolt of cheap white bleached cotton with a tag on it stating the state retail price at seventy cents to the meter. I asked the manager how much it cost to make. He told me twenty cents.

There is no free rate of exchange between rubles and dollars. The official rate is four rubles for one dollar but tourists are given ten rubles for one dollar. I have used the ten-rubles-to-one-dollar rate throughout this book, as it seems to be more realistic, especially in consumer goods.

At an automobile plant the director showed me a bus which he said sold for $2,000, including a profit of around five per cent. Beside it was a passenger car which he told me sells for $4,000—probably several times what it costs to build. And of course the profits of these plants do not go to build consumer-goods factories but chiefly to heavy industry, the backbone of the Soviet arms industry.

One reason for these exorbitant prices is to keep down demand for articles in short supply, a function which they no doubt successfully perform. However, I am inclined to believe that foreigners sometimes exaggerate the effect of these high prices on the Soviet consumers. Until very recently few of them had seen a washing machine or a refrigerator. The idea of owning a private car was reserved only for those who might one day reach the very top of the highly paid professions in politics, science or the arts.

Today they are building nearly four hundred thousand refrigerators and somewhat more washing machines each year—hardly a tenth of our production, but they are to be seen in shop windows together with a hundred other luxuries the Soviet population had scarcely dreamed of a decade ago. During the Seven-Year Plan production is scheduled to increase to two million refrigerators and four million washing machines annually. While the prices are still high for the average income, who knows how soon they may come down? At all events they are a far more tangible incentive to working harder and earning more or studying harder and getting a better job than the vague promises of Joseph Stalin about the happy future life. To the humblest window-shopper they are infinitely more stimulating than the wooden hams and sausages that adorned the shop win-

dows when I used to walk about Moscow in the last years
of the war.

During Stalin's rule he demanded, as I have said, the
most immense sacrifices from his people in order to build
up Soviet heavy industry—"the basis of the entire Soviet
economy," as the Soviet slogan runs. He made only the
rarest concessions to the longing of the Soviet people for a
few of the most insignificant luxuries. One of these concessions was the cosmetics industry run by Molotov's wife,
Zhemshchuzhina, and before the war Soviet towns were
studded with shops selling cheap lipstick, perfume, toilet
soaps and rouge. Economists attributed this concession not
to Stalin's kindness of heart but chiefly to the need to drain
off excess spending power among the middle- and upper-
income groups.

During the last years of his rule Stalin made further concessions, and shops were opened to sell furs (heretofore
exported), clocks and clothing and even cocktails. But
these too were concentrated only in the major cities. Their
chief purpose was, I believe, partly to impress foreigners
and partly to demonstrate to the population what they
might have if they worked just a little harder and longer.

When Stalin died, his first successor in the premiership,
Malenkov, urged that the consumer get a better break, and
he argued that the consumer-goods industry must be greatly
expanded. But even before the factories for turning out
the goods came into production, Malenkov was removed.
Khrushchev and his supporters decided to slow down the
increase and restore heavy industry to first place in their
list of priorities.

In a long talk I had with Alexander N. Kosygin, whom
I had known during the war and who is now head of the
State Planning Commission, Gosplan, which decides what

plants are to be built and what goods produced, I recalled to him that when we last met he had been head of the consumer-goods industries. Did his recent appointment to the senior planning organ mean that now at last these industries would get a better break?

"Not at all," he replied solemnly. "Such matters are not decided by personalities but by the Communist Party Congress. The Twentieth Party Congress has decreed that heavy industry shall continue to predominate, and that is the way I shall run Gosplan."

I called attention to current plans for reducing working hours to forty-one hours a week. I said that in the United States many working people would prefer working overtime in order to earn extra income to buy more goods for their families. Would not the Soviet worker also prefer to continue to work longer hours and have more consumer goods? I asked. But Kosygin did not look at the problem that way. "The party," he said, "has promised the workers shorter hours. We must fulfill this pledge."

When Mr. Khrushchev speaks of raising the Soviet living standard to the American level within his lifetime, it is difficult to believe that this is more than another propaganda hoax for world consumption and a glittering mirage to spur his people to greater efforts. I believe that he sincerely means to raise the living standard very substantially to a level he considers comparable to our own, but it will be quite different from what we know. Complying with the Marxist concept of collectivism, it will emphasize collective entertainment and recreation—relatively few automobiles but improved mass transportation.

The present Communist dogma provides that only the upper crust of Soviet society will be able to seek their personal pleasures individually in private cars. The rest will be taken to their "culture and rest" collectively in communal autobuses. However, I found little evidence that the Slav soul has yet been bent to conform to this doctrinaire preference for collective living. On the contrary, everywhere I saw signs of a deep-seated longing for individual self-expression and privacy—from the crowds of university students looking wistfully at the foreign tourists' Volkswagens to the senior State Planning official hurrying through our Saturday luncheon so that he could get out to tend his little private garden plot in the suburbs.

Which of these two ways of life will in the long run prevail there is no way of telling. But for the foreseeable future I see no evidence that Khrushchev is prepared to sacrifice to the longings of Soviet consumers the expansion of heavy industry with which to make the weapons he thinks he needs.

CHAPTER FIVE

Khrushchev's Concrete Houses

"STALIN SPARED NO ONE in his drive to build socialist industry," a high Russian official told me recently. "He demanded the greatest sacrifices both from himself and from the people." In no aspect of life did Stalin demand a greater sacrifice than in housing. During the early years of his rule, in his single-minded drive to create an industrial base for the Soviet Union he seriously neglected housing. Though apartments were built they did not begin to keep pace with the growth of the urban population caused by industrialization.

Moscow today is a city of five and a half million inhabitants; when I first visited it in 1926, it was a sprawling city of two millions. People called it an overgrown village. Aside from the imposing Kremlin its most attractive features were the pale-yellow Empire-style public buildings and private homes, many of them designed by the Italian architect Gilliardi after the great fire of 1812 during the Napoleonic invasion. Public conveyances still included the horse-drawn droshkies which rumbled along its narrow cobblestone streets.

Before the war started, Stalin had begun to beautify and modernize his capital. Many of the Empire buildings were pulled down to make way for enormous asphalt squares and eighty-yard-wide boulevards. In the center of the city a number of monumental apartment buildings were constructed to impress visitors from the provinces and abroad.

When I left the Soviet Union after the war many of the cities of European Russia from Kiev to Stalingrad were largely charred ruins and Stalin was forced to devote considerable resources and energy to repairing the war damage. He also resumed his program for beautifying the capital and erected seven ornate pinnacled skyscrapers that rose white and gleaming above the skyline. But meantime behind them the charming little yellow nineteenth-century houses, which had not been painted or repaired since the Revolution, were crumbling to ruins, while their occupants strove desperately to keep the wind and the snow and the rain from seeping through walls and roofs.

The standard space requirement established by the Soviet health authorities is about one hundred square feet per person. But even in favored Moscow this has never been met. Mayor Bobrovnikov told me that the average Muscovite now occupies a space less than seventy square feet. In some provincial towns I visited it is as low as fifty square feet—scarcely more than the size of a double bed. (It should, however, be said that in computing floor space the Soviets exclude bathrooms, kitchens and corridors.) It has been estimated that the average floor space per person in America is four times as great.

Overcrowding is not only a threat to the population's physical health. I am told that the Soviet custom of squeezing families of three and four into one room creates a severe nervous strain. The distracted mother returns from teaching school to find several other weary women crowding around the single stove in the communal kitchen preparing supper. The tired father returns from a long day in the office or factory to find his small children running around the single family room. The student son home from his stint in the factory seeks in vain for a quiet corner where he can study his correspondence course in engineering. Soviet authorities do not publish statistics on nervous disorders but if these are not high it is a tribute to the Russian's phlegmatic nature.

When Khrushchev took over in the Kremlin he recognized that only the most drastic action could alleviate the growing shortage of housing. His first step was to triple and even quadruple building programs for housing. His second step was to scrap all plans for more ornate skyscrapers and to chastise the Soviet architects for the wasteful, extravagant and gaudy buildings they had designed to comply with Stalin's tastes. There was a touch of irony in this scolding, for it was in Kiev, where Khrushchev had been Stalin's satrap, that some of the most extravagantly ornate Stalinesque building I saw during my recent trip had been built. Whole streets were lined with ten- and twelve-story apartment buildings topped with crenellated turrets and baroque balustrades and walled by brilliant mosaics, Gothic columns and Oriental balconies.

Khrushchev told the architects that from now on all new apartment buildings would be divested of "superfluous embellishments" and every ruble in the housing program used to increase floor space. He called on builders and engineers to work out building methods which would provide the greatest number of apartments for the least cost, with the greatest speed and without interfering with heavy industry's needs for building materials in short supply.

Since steel is scarce in the Soviet Union, the builders turned to concrete. After some hasty experimentation a system of prefabricated, standardized concrete slabs, panels and reinforced columns and girders was devised and builders all over the country were instructed to adopt it. Wherever I went throughout my trip I saw plants being built to make the prefabricated concrete slabs, panels and other forms for the new building program.

The efficiency of the new system for speedy building was described to me by one of Moscow's senior architects. He stated that by using prefabricated concrete forms the same number of construction workers who once built one and a half millon square meters of space in a year are presently putting up almost double that quantity. This included the manpower in the plants where the concrete slabs are made. Whereas the city once employed up to three hundred persons to put up a building, now only fifty or sixty, he told me, are engaged.

In many cities I was shown through new apartment buildings being constructed by the new methods. In the cities of European Russia I saw rows upon rows of chunky concrete buildings rising unadorned and unrelieved by a single frill, their hastily mortared, monotonous paneled façades in striking contrast to the extravaganzas of Stalin's day. Though in some places a few attempts had been made to break up the monotony by a variety of tiled facings, these were seldom successful. You can't make marble out of Communist concrete. In Central Asia the dullness had been relieved by clever use of color and stuccoed Asiatic decorations.

One city of the dozen or more I visited stood out in sharp contrast to the rest—Leningrad.

During the war, Leningrad had withstood a seige by the

Germans lasting over nine hundred days, during much of which the city was completely surrounded and cut off from the rest of Russia except for a slender supply route laid across the frozen Lake Ladoga in the wintertime. As a result of artillery fire the city had been severely damaged. In all, some twenty-seven million square yards of housing had been damaged, eighteen million of which had been destroyed.

German artillery had not been the only destructive element in Leningrad. Ever since the Revolution, when the Communists abandoned Peter the Great's new capital and returned to Moscow, little or nothing had been done to maintain the ancient palaces and monuments. Even before the war the paint had faded and peeled from the façades. Cornices and columns had disintegrated and broken. The great windows of the Winter Palace and the old Admiralty were blank and empty, staring vacantly onto the slowly disintegrating cobblestone streets Peter himself had laid out. A traveler seeing Leningrad got the impression that it was a half-abandoned city.

Under Khrushchev, the architects of Leningrad had been exempt from the general decree to build nothing but the plainest apartment buildings. The Institute for the Restoration of Historic Monuments, which has its headquarters in Leningrad, was instructed to rebuild the center of the city precisely as it had existed prior to the Revolution. Where façades had been damaged they were repaired just as they had appeared in the heyday of the Czars. Where whole buildings had been destroyed, the original plans were dug out of the archives and the buildings re-erected according to the original architect's design.

Whether damaged or not, the buildings in the historic parts of the city were repaired and repainted in the pale

yellows and pastel blues for which it had been famous in
the nineteenth century. The streets were repaved, the em-
bankment along the Neva River was restored and dozens
of drainage canals were cleaned up and their banks relined
with stone. Even the interiors of the palaces were carefully
restored, and once more bright-colored curtains hung in
the long-vacant windows.

When I revisited Leningrad the white nights of the Arctic
summer were beginning. Late in the evening when I returned from the famous Mariinsky Theater, the sky was
still lit with a luminous blue glow. On the Cathedral of St.
Isaac and the obelisk above the Admiralty subdued flood-
lights lit up the gold domes and spires. By day the cheer-
fully colored façades brightened the magnificent squares for
which St. Petersburg had been famous.

Outside of town on the Gulf of Finland I visited again
the palace of Peterhof, begun by Peter and finished by Cath-
erine the Great. During the siege it had been totally destroyed by the Germans but it too had been almost completely restored. Although it was before the summer season
the authorities had turned on the famous fountains for my
wife and me to admire.

I wish I could say as much for the other cities I visited
in the Soviet Union. Though some of the historic buildings
of Moscow—including, of course, the Kremlin—have also
been restored, the newer buildings whether of the Stalin
era or Khrushchev's, lack the taste and the atmosphere I
had remembered from my earliest visit in 1926.

Another exception to the drabness of Khrushchev's housing which I unexpectedly found both in Leningrad and in
other Russian cities was the churches and monasteries. Ever
since the Revolution the churches of Russia—there were
eight hundred in Moscow alone—were allowed to crumble

and decay. Those which were closed or converted into museums were, like other Soviet buildings, poorly maintained if at all. The church authorities who controlled those still in use had neither the funds nor the access to scarce building materials and paint to keep the buildings up.

Recently the Soviet authorities have set aside funds to restore a number of the more historic churches each year as national architectural monuments. The ecclesiastical authorities have also been encouraged to restore the few churches still functioning. The materials for their restoration have been made available but must be paid for by the congregations. In Moscow I saw several former churches surrounded by scaffolding on which masons and painters were working, and I was told that this year between ten and twenty churches will be restored in the capital.

In one respect, the housing of the Stalin and the Khrushchev eras is alike—the shoddiness of the workmanship and the poor quality of the ever present concrete. In the Stalinesque buildings many cornices had long since crumbled. Everywhere black streaks ran down the façades. In some buildings that had hardly been finished, the concrete staircases were already chipped and the balustrades unsteady. Inside the apartments fixtures were already loose. Floors had buckled and window frames had shrunken away from the walls.

The builders and architects explained to me that since it was impossible to get seasoned lumber and since they could not wait till it dried lest they fall behind on their plan, it had become standard practice to repair all apartment house floors, windows and doors one year after they had been built. Whether the repairmen would turn up on schedule was problematical.

During my conversation with Mr. Kosygin of the State

Planning Commission, I suggested that speed and frugality with building materials had caused considerable sacrifice in quality. He replied that his commission was constantly keeping a vigilant eye on the quality of construction. And he added, "If you had seen it five years ago you would note a considerable improvement today."

Several years ago, Mr. Khrushchev in a speech to builders reminded them that in Czarist days he had been a plumber too. "The plumbing you people are putting in today," he said, "is worse than anything we did forty-five years ago." What I saw of Soviet plumbing bore out his criticism.

The poor workmanship of Soviet builders is in striking contrast with their skill in other fields and illustrates one important aspect of the Soviet planned economy—the system of priorities. When a project is undertaken to build a sputnik or erect a steel plant it is given so high a priority both for materials and for skills that the finished product is equal to the best world practice, If, on the other hand, a project is undertaken to build a house for working people, it gets so low a priority for materials and skilled labor that the results are such as I have described above.

In Karaganda in the heart of the Kazakh steppe I watched a crew of women laying brick to line a blast furnace with the same precision one would find in the best American steel mill. A mile or two away another crew of women was laying brick for a new dwelling of such shoddy quality that only a thick layer of plaster could hide the defects.

In contrast to the hasty and poor workmanship and the plainness of the architecture, I was impressed by the efforts of Soviet city planners to plant as much greenery as possible, not only in extensive parks but along the wide streets and boulevards, and especially in the open spaces that they have wisely left between the apartment buildings for children's playgrounds and recreation areas. In Stalingrad, for example, the mayor told me that his aim was to provide nearly twenty square yards of green area to every inhabitant of the city. His purpose was to reduce the effect of the dust storms raised by prevailing winds from the desert east of the Volga and to increase rainfall within the city—or, as he put it in the new Soviet jargon, to improve the city's "microclimate."

City planners have also used their dictatorial powers extensively to make the most of available real estate for the purpose of improving a city's layout and transportation system. The suburbs of Moscow, for example, have been built up in accordance with a single integrated plan. Each new community is well laid out, with a generous allocation of open spaces—including playgrounds and neatly planted boulevards—between buildings, and is also directly connected with the heart of the city by broad radial streets extending from the Kremlin itself.

In Stalingrad I was shown photographs of the factories, lumberyards and dump heaps which once lined the river front for many miles. Since the war most of these have been removed, and a wide promenade now stretches several miles along the river in the center of town. Two main traffic arteries, one for passenger traffic and the other for trucks, are being built through the city, parallel to the river.

In Leningrad Mayor Smirnov told me that due to high humidity, much cloudy weather and the absence of strong winds, smog was becoming a serious problem. To combat this the city council is requiring a number of industries contributing to air pollution, such as coal-burning metallurgical plants, either to convert to gas or to install filters on their stacks. A number of smoke-producing industries, including some chemical plants, are being moved out of the city entirely.

Another of the extensive powers which Soviet municipal authorities use to solve their problems is the power to forbid new migrants to move into the cities from rural areas. The mayors of Moscow, Leningrad and Kiev told me that in order to prevent too rapid growth of their cities, the police refused to give residence permits which are required by law to newcomers, thus in effect making all three cities "closed" areas for rural migrants. Furthermore, despite the immense expansion of industry in the current Seven-Year Plan, Moscow is not permitting new factories to be built in the city; in fact, a number of heavy metallurgical plants are being moved out. In Leningrad too no new industries are to be permitted. To expand existing industries, the authorities are counting on substantial increases in labor productivity and on the increased labor force resulting from natural growth.

To provide the additional services contemplated under the Seven-Year Plan, both Moscow and Leningrad are adopting a program first devised in Scandinavia, of so-called "satellite cities." These communities, varying from 45,000 to 70,000 population, are to be located twenty or thirty miles beyond the city limits and will contain chiefly consumer industries, such as electrical-appliance plants, garment factories and construction materials plants, for the main city. About twenty-five miles northeast of Moscow I saw bulldozers, graders and giant shovels clearing ground for one of the first of these "satellites," of which seven or eight are currently planned.

Despite the strenuous efforts demanded by Khrushchev for a rapid improvement in living space, it is estimated that it will take many years before even the minimum requirements are met. The mayors of Moscow and Leningrad stated that by 1965 they hoped to have the required one hundred square feet of living space per person. But in Stalingrad, which was completely destroyed by the Germans, the mayor said it would take considerably longer to reach even this modest level, and in some towns in Kazakhstan minimum requirements will not be met until the seventies.

On the southwest edge of Moscow one of the largest of all Soviet housing developments is now under construction. I was taken to see an apartment in what the city architect described as an experimental building. The apartment was occupied by another architect, whose wife showed me through it with considerable pride. It had two small bedrooms, one occupied by herself and her husband and the other by her daughter and son-in-law. Between them they shared a living-dining room which was about twelve by twenty-four feet. Off the entrance corridor was a small bathroom and a kitchenette with a two-burner gas stove and a small wooden kitchen cabinet. The kitchen had no refrigerator and I saw no sign of any other kitchen equipment except a few pots and pans. The apartment was heated from a municipal heating plant, with hot water running through concrete radiators which the architect's wife assured me kept the rooms warm in the coldest of Moscow's winter days.

Despite Mr. Khrushchev's recently publicized boasts about the mechanization of Moscow's modern apartments and the lavish equipment he suggested they contained, this apartment—which was certainly not the least modern of Moscow's new units and was probably among the best—would hardly have been considered adequate by an American housewife. However, I am sure that the architect's wife, inured by decades to crowding with several other families into a single apartment, was wholly sincere when she told me how delighted she was with it. The same, I am sure, can be said of the tens of thousands of others who each year are moving into these new communities.

One feature of urban crowding is the tendency of the lucky recipient of a new apartment to share his good fortune not only with his immediate family but with married children, in-laws and grandparents. The result is that a new apartment designed for a single couple soon resembles a tribal camp with stray relatives tucked away into every available corner.

Occasionally I ran into more sophisticated Muscovites who complained that the designers of these new apartment house projects ignored the hunger of the average Russian for a little beauty, individuality and privacy in his surroundings. "They are utterly soulless," one of them told a city housing official in my presence. "I am living in a single old apartment with three other families, but I prefer that to any of these concrete beehives you are building."

This craving for more privacy and more individuality which the Russians feel so strongly is being demonstrated by the private houses being built, especially in the smaller cities. In contrast to Moscow and Leningrad these have plenty of semiurban real estate for private housing plots and gardens. Americans are often surprised to find that a very large percentage of Soviet citizens own their own homes. On the collective farms, where about half the population live, practically all housing is privately built and owned. In the smaller cities I visited, from twenty-five to fifty per cent of the housing is private.

In each of these towns districts have been set aside by the city planners for what is called "individual housing." In Stalinabad in Central Asia I was taken to one of these areas and told I might inspect any private house I chose. Selecting at random a gate in a high wooden wall, I rang the doorbell and a moment later was greeted by a local Tadzhik dressed in silk pajamas. When he had recovered from the shock of a large party of foreigners and officials invading his home he welcomed us with obvious delight. His wife, an unusually handsome woman, barefoot but clothed in a gaily printed cotton dress, led us to a big veranda, where the family of a dozen or more were seated on a raised platform around a huge bowl of pilaf—rice mixed with bits of mutton.

Our host, Mr. Khudododoev (no relation, he told me, of the Prime Minister, Mr. Dodokhudoev) brought out European chairs for us to sit on. The veranda faced a garden of flowers and fruit trees surrounded by a high fence. At the bottom of the garden was a small four-room house occupied, our host said, by two married sons and their families.

The main house consisted of a living room, four bedrooms and a "winter kitchen." During the hot summer months in Central Asia all cooking is done on small stoves in the garden. With special pride Mr. Khudododoev pointed out an electric refrigerator. He opened it to reveal that in addition to a leg of mutton it was crammed with bottles of beer.

"I am a master brewer," he explained proudly.

He said that his wife had designed the house herself but that he had hired a master carpenter to supervise the construction, which was of wood. The actual work had been done by himself and his family, which includes three sons, two daughters, two daughters-in-law and a dozen grandchildren.

He said that he earned a salary of between $170 and $180

per month, depending on how well the city brewery fulfilled its prescribed plan. His wife, a former Communist Party official, received a pension of $120 because of an illness which had permanently incapacitated her. In addition, the family shared the incomes of two married sons and, of course, of their wives, making a total of five salaries and a substantial pension.

It had cost him $3,900 to build the house, he told me, and he had made use of the regular government loan of $1,000 available to individual home builders at a low interest rate. He added that he had long since repaid the loan. The house belongs to him permanently, and the land on which it was built, though it belongs technically to the government, is on a more or less perpetual lease, for which he pays a small sum annually. The city had installed both running water and sewage, for which he pays a nominal tax. He is free to sell the house or bequeath it to his children. A city official who was present stated that for tax purposes and insurance the house is assessed a given value. However, if the owner wants to sell he can ask as much as he thinks he can get for it. "The city never interferes in such private deals," the mayor told me.

Extricating ourselves from the hospitable arms of our host and hostess turned out to be a far more difficult problem than getting into their property. First we had to taste the pilaf and, of course, the beer and the soft drinks made by the host's brewery. Then a series of photographs with our Polaroid camera had to be taken, with the stout mother of the owner as the central figure. Finally came an exchange of gifts. I received an embroidered Central Asian skullcap. In return I gave our host a ball-point pen. As we left, the stout mother gave my wife a motherly hug and kissed her warmly on both cheeks.

Though the urban individual housing we saw in Stalinabad consisted almost exclusively of small bungalows, their gaily painted shutters and carved decorations on window and door frames demonstrated that craving for individuality which the huge apartment houses do so little to satisfy. Besides, as Mr. Khudododoev pointed out, life without a garden in the semitropical areas of Central Asia and southern Russia is no life at all.

On a number of collective farms I visited I also saw the modern peasant housing that is going up. At an agricultural and industrial exhibition in Kiev I was shown a number of model peasant houses designed by Soviet engineers to assist farmers in improving the traditional log-cabin type of construction that has heretofore prevailed everywhere in the villages. Five model peasant homes were shown, varying in price from $2,400 for a frame building to $4,500 for a one-family brick house. Cut-out sections of the walls showed prospective builders exactly how the walls were constructed and insulated.

In the villages, running water and sewage are still almost completely nonexistent and outhouses are everywhere standard equipment. Despite these lacks, many of the villages I saw were electrified either from a regional or nearby municipal power line or by their own generator plants. Peasants desiring to build their homes, it was explained, often build them themselves. In Siberian villages I saw young men sawing great logs while their wives carried hods of mud and mortar to caulk the chinks. In some cases, state or collective farms have organized building teams which for a price will build a peasant his house. But the most ordinary way, I was told, is for the builder to enlist the assistance of his neighbors. In such cases the neighbors are remunerated only when the house is complete, at a celebration similar to our housewarmings which is known in Russia as "watering the home" and where vodka is the principal liquid. In one or two instances in new construction sites in Siberia I was also shown "co-operative houses" with several apartments each, which two or three families build together.

Despite the large part played by private housing and the encouragement that municipal and rural authorities are giving to it on instructions from Moscow, I had the impression that this method is more an expedient than a permanent feature of the new Khrushchev form of socialism. Private ownership, according to Marxist doctrine, is a remnant of the capitalist state. The future belongs to collective effort and collective ownership. The concession to private building is therefore only a means of satisfying one of the most crying needs of Soviet society and may be tolerated only as long as the housing shortage is not overcome.

Municipal housing authorities in Stalingrad, Alma-Ata, Karaganda and other provincial towns told me that in the next few years the urban individual home-building program is to be cut back in favor of public housing. However, the attachment of owners to their little houses and gardens is strong and likely to grow. What may happen someday when the private-property instincts of homeowners come into conflict with the decisions of municipal planners or with party doctrines is anyone's guess.

Not long ago at a vaudeville show in Moscow a performer recited a poem which would never have been tolerated under Stalin. The theme was that he, a loyal Soviet citizen, was marching proudly and determinedly toward Communism, but, he added, there were some nails sticking through the soles of his shoes.

The current Khrushchev housing program is one of the best illustrations of how the present leadership is making a determined effort to reduce the pain caused by nails in people's shoes. Housing today is still a major problem. The majority of Soviet citizens will not have adequate apartments for five, ten or even fifteen years to come, even according to their own modest standards. To thousands of Muscovites still living in damp cellars or ramshackle shacks without sewage or running water, in the shadow of Stalin's ostentatious skyscrapers, the new beehive apartments on the outskirts of the city represent only a faint light at the end of a long tunnel. But the light, they can see, is real and not the intangible will-o'-the-wisp that Stalin held up to them for decades. Many will have to wait patiently for years before this nail is pulled from their shoe. But patience is a quality for which the Russians have been famous throughout history.

CHAPTER SIX

Stalin's Bread
and Khrushchev's Butter

ONE OF THE MOST persistent beliefs about the Soviet Union has been that the collective-farm and state farm system can never solve Russia's chronic food shortage. This was one of the ideas I was particularly interested in exploring during my recent trip, because inadequate food resources can not only retard national development but also make military adventures impossible.

Although Czarist Russia exported large quantities of grain, it suffered periodically from widespread local famines. During the early years of the Communist regime there were serious shortages even of bread. In 1921–22 there was a major famine in two of the principal agricultural areas. In the winter of 1932–33 as many as ten million peasants starved to death, it is estimated, partly as a result of drought and partly because of their refusal to accept Stalin's forced collectivization. During the war, Stalin's requests for American assistance included not only arms and industrial materials but sugar, meat, lard and even flour for the civilian population as well as the troops. Even so there was serious undernourishment among elements of the population.

On this visit I found that the Soviet people are no longer in danger of starving. Though meat and dairy products are often hard to come by, the collective system is producing bread, potatoes, cabbage, cucumbers and other basic staples. The problem I found Khrushchev tackling is not famine but the monotonous, unbalanced diet Russians have always had to put up with. He promised to add butter to the bread.

Khrushchev is the first prominent Communist in history who has had personal experience with farming. He told me that he started working at the age of seven as a shepherd on a large Ukrainian farm belonging to a German. Now for the first time the Kremlin has a leader who understands not only how peasants think but why they work—or don't work.

When he came to power he recognized that the collective farms would never produce efficiently if they were not given some incentive. He promptly eased the system whereby peasants were forced to turn over most of their crops to the state at less-than-cost prices.

"Up to a few years ago," one provincial agricultural official told me candidly, "the Soviet collective farmer had no reason to grow better crops or produce higher yields." But when Khrushchev raised prices by as much as fifty per cent there was an almost immediate increase in agricultural production.

The problem of improving the Soviet diet was a more difficult matter. Soon after assuming power, Khrushchev promised the Soviet population more milk, butter and meat. He knew what Stalin refused to recognize: that if you don't feed a cow enough it won't produce milk. The task was to grow the fodder for the increased numbers of cattle, pigs and poultry he had promised. Corn had long been grown in the Ukraine and North Caucasus, but in limited quantities. As early as 1953, the year Stalin died, Khrushchev urged its planting in northern areas where it would not mature to grain but could be used for silage. Then in 1955 he sent one of his leading agricultural experts, Vladimir V. Matskevich, to the United States to find out how to produce quick-maturing, high-yield hybrid and double-hybrid corn. Thereafter corn production in the Soviet Union was greatly increased. At present, fifty million acres are in corn, two thirds for silage and the rest for grain.

The Ukraine was traditionally the Soviet Union's breadbasket. Khrushchev now had to look elsewhere for arable land on which to grow the grain that the corn had supplanted there. With characteristic boldness, his eye turned to the arid plains of eastern Siberia and Kazakhstan, which heretofore had produced only sparse steppe grazing for sheep and cattle. When he announced his scheme, agricultural experts around the world predicted in alarm, "Dust bowl!"

But Mr. Khrushchev's boldness should not, as has sometimes been done, be confused with brashness. Only after his scientists and agronomists had carefully studied local soil conditions, rainfall and other factors was the choice made. Agricultural specialists were sent to similar areas in the United States and Canada—the notorious dust bowl country—and they meticulously investigated the conditions.

Only after these investigations was the decision taken to plow up the so-called virgin lands. At Kustanai in northern Kazakhstan I visited a typical virgin-lands state farm. Mr. Mikhailov, the director of the Viktorov state farm, is a Ukrainian by origin. Like most good Yankee farmers, he is taciturn and very sparing of words. He has managed farms all over European Russia. But the Kustanai farm, he told me, was by all odds the most challenging. "I guess it's the scale on which we operate," he explained, waving his hand across thousands of acres of rolling steppe, all green with young wheat.

The farm had a little over one hundred thousand acres in plow. In its best year in 1956 it had produced an average yield of nearly thirty bushels of grain per acre. But in 1957 and again in 1958 when rainfall had been slight it had fallen to an average of only a third as much. This year, he said, if he got one of two good rainfalls before the middle of July he hoped to reap about fifteen bushels per acre, which he considered entirely satisfactory.

Later Mr. Khrushchev told me that if the virgin lands produced three average harvests in five years, the project would be a success. In the five years since he started the program, he added, he had had two good crops and one average one, which netted the Soviet state a "profit" of nearly two billion dollars over and above the investment in machinery, farm buildings and maintenance.

Mr. Mikhailov told me he had come to Kustanai in the spring of 1955—after the virgin-lands program was well under way. The "farm" allotted to him had been a naked prairie when he drove the first stake for his first tent. That year had been devoted to plowing and preparing the soil for the next year's sowing, and to building the first shelters for his equipment and workers.

Manpower was, of course, his biggest problem. Despite Mr. Khrushchev's appeal to the youth of the western Soviet Union to "go east" and pioneer the new territories, there was considerable reluctance to follow his advice. Komsomol, the Communist youth organization, had "recruited" a substantial number of young people, but, Mr. Mikhailov complained, they were almost entirely from urban areas and had only industrial experience. "They had never seen a plow," he said. Evidently when they eventually did see them in the virgin lands they were unimpressed, and almost half of them eventually returned to European Russia.

After that recruiting efforts were directed toward young married couples and people with experience in farming. The result has been a considerable decrease in labor turnover. At present the farm employs about 660 workers making up about 420 households. The farm bookkeeper, a husky, good-looking and energetic young woman, told me proudly that the women outnumber the men.

Today the farm comprises several small villages and a half-dozen field camps where the workers live in boxcarlike trailers out in the fields during the summer season. The main village is a neatly laid-out community in which the majority of workers have built their own small wooden houses surrounded by well-tended garden plots.

One of the houses I visited was occupied by a couple with two children. Both parents and a teen-age son were on the farm's payroll. The house, consisting of three rooms and a small cooking alcove, was spotlessly clean and was decorated with colored prints, photographs and an ikon.

A nursery for young children whose parents were working in the fields had recently been finished. A score of them, dressed in red-and-white pinafores and large hats to shield them from the brilliant desert sun, greeted me with bouquets of wild flowers. Nearby was a hospital with about twenty-five beds, including a maternity ward which, I was told, was in constant use. Three doctors and twenty-four nurses were available for the entire farm. The hospital also was equipped with laboratory, a clinic, an X-ray room and a heat therapy ward. I asked the chief doctor, a pretty blond girl in her late twenties, what sort of water supply the hospital had. "We carry it from a well," she told me. Neither the hospital

In the first place, the entire farm had been carefully surveyed by a special commission which had determined which sections would be plowed and which, because of the sandy soil, must be left in pasture. Practically all tillable soil had already been brought under cultivation and only a few additional fields might be plowed. If they desired to plow any more they would have to obtain the commission's special permission. In some light-soil areas the wheat is sown in 100-yard-wide strips, leaving equally wide strips in grass between them.

In the second place, they explained, while the summers in Kazakhstan are dry, winter snowfall is considerable. Agronomists had calculated that if methods could be devised to preserve the total precipitation, including the snow, it would theoretically provide enough moisture to produce average yields up to well over thirty bushels per acre. Though they could not hope to accomplish this, they had devised a number of methods—some of them copied from Canadian and American farmers—to retain the moisture of the snowfall. One method included plowing the first snowfall into ridges, thus preventing the snow from being blown off into gullies or, as I had myself often observed on the Union Pacific Railroad, into railroad cuts and uncultivatable draws. A second method of retaining moisture and preventing the breaking up of the topsoil was an ingenious instrument which broke up the subsoil without disturbing the snow-retaining stubble.

But the most important protection which they used against erosion was to plow the soil only once in four years and then with a blade which did not turn over the topsoil. In the intervening years the ground is only disked and weeded. This method, they acknowledged, they had borrowed from Canadian and American agronomists.

As yet the farms in the virgin-soil areas are only beginning to grapple with crop rotation problems. Eventually, however, they plan to leave land fallow once in every four or five years. For the first time this year a comparatively small area of the Viktorov farm is lying fallow to recuperate its fertility.

When one compares the haphazard cultivating practices which at least in part gave rise to our own dust bowl problems with the care and caution Soviet agronomists are using on the new lands of Kazakhstan, it is difficult to escape the impression that a similar catastrophe is far less likely to overtake them. On the other hand, such a possibility cannot be definitely excluded and sharp variations in yields depending on rainfall must be expected. Later in a discussion of the problem with a well-known Soviet geologist I was told that in his opinion further experience was required before the danger of serious wind erosion could be dismissed.

Mr. Khrushchev, however, is confident the project will not end in disaster. "The skeptics are already blushing for shame," he told me.

Mr. Khrushchev's other efforts to improve the food supply are also meeting with some success. In Stalin's time the Communist cry was to increase the number of cattle. Today Khrushchev is demanding that feeding be improved and more attention be paid to breeding.

The Soviet Minister of Agriculture took me to an experimental state farm on the outskirts of Moscow where black-and-white Holsteins were producing up to twenty thousand pounds of milk a year. Of course, these were top producers, but even the average were giving twelve thousand pounds. At a collective farm near Kiev the chairman told me his cows were producing eight thousand pounds of milk per year. (A good herd in New York State will average ten thousand pounds per cow.) But of course this is well above the average and on the steppes of Kazakhstan, where the grass is sparse and poor, cows yield little more than three or four thousand pounds a year.

I was also impressed by the efforts to improve livestock strains by better breeding methods. In my talks with Khrushchev he pointed out that the Soviet scientists had made considerable progress in artificial insemination as early as the 1930s. However, he said, these advances had never been put to practical use; in fact, American farmers had made much better use of them than the Soviets, who, he claimed, had developed them. Now, however, he was insisting that these methods be put to service to improve breeds.

At an agricultural exhibit near Kiev I watched a cattle show which takes place several times a day for the benefit of visiting collective farmers. Specimens of various breeds of cattle were led into a ring, where an expert pointed out the good and bad points of each and explained the advantages of each breed, whether for beef or for milk— Holsteins from Denmark, Ziementhalers from Switzerland, red-and-white Ukrainians and several varieties of Soviet steppe cattle. What impressed me was that Khrushchev is introducing such advanced methods for the first time into Soviet agricultural practices.

In fact, during my talks with him he mentioned our American extension system of helping farmers make use of new scientific methods and said that he intended to copy our methods. The scientific institutes in the Soviet Union studying agronomy and animal husbandry, he complained, were spending huge government subsidies on experiments which were not being put into practice. From now on, he told me, these institutes would have to pay their way by developing farm practices which collective and state farms could pay for and readily use to raise yields and production.

In Central Asia I found evidence that his insistence was producing results. There scientific institutes were studying the specific problems of local farms and even doing experimental work on a contract basis for individual collective and state farms. For example, they were developing better cotton strains to meet specific soil conditions, which, after thorough testing, they would sell to nearby cotton collectives.

Another innovation of Khrushchev was to get rid of the machine tractor stations, the centralized tractor plants which served collective farms on a contract basis. The stations embodied a basic principle of Marxism that the "means of production" be kept in government hands and out of the control of the semi-independent collective farms. During Stalin's regime it had been proposed that turning over the machines to the farmers would increase efficiency and reduce bureaucracy. However, Stalin, always suspicious of the peasantry, had rejected any such concession.

It was characteristic of the peasant-born Khrushchev to reverse the decision and to sell to the collective farms the machinery they had been renting from the stations. He even loaned the farms money to buy the equipment. Today most Soviet farms control their machinery directly and, from what they told me, are making good use of their new independence. Whether abandoning this powerful lever of control over the farmers will lead to demands for even greater independence remains to be seen.

During Stalin's lifetime a scheme was put forward to convert the Soviet agricultural community into a series of giant agricultural enterprises by combining several farms into a single *agrogorod,* or agricultural town. The scheme was particularly advocated by Khrushchev and when it was rejected by Stalin Soviet specialists interpreted it as a sign of Khrushchev's waning influence. Although it has never been revived in precisely the form in which Khrushchev presented it originally, there has for the past several years been a vigorous drive to reduce the number of individual collectives by combining two or three into a single one—without, however, building the communal rural apartment houses that the original scheme had envisaged.

From over two hundred thousand farms, the number has been steadily reduced to less than sixty thousand at the present time, Minister Matskevich informed me. The official reason for this reduction of numbers and increase in size is to increase efficiency. However, I have the impression that a second reason is to wean the peasant gradually from his attachment to a single small community and make him part of a much larger organization, with the eventual aim of making him, like the city factory worker, a part of a giant machine.

The same tendency is demonstrated in still another farm reform introduced by Khrushchev. From the earliest days of the collectives, farmers had been paid according to a fictitious unit called the workday. To conform to standard Soviet practice of paying by piecework, every job on the farm was evaluated in terms of workdays. Some jobs constituted half a workday, others two or three workdays. In a year one collective farmer might accumulate up to four or five hundred workday pay units according to which the farm's profits were distributed.

This year Khrushchev abolished the workday unit and put all farmers on a straight monthly-salary basis, with a proviso that at the end of the year undistributed farm profits would be shared proportionately to the wages earned. The official reason for this change, as a farm director in Alma-Ata explained to me, was to simplify the bookkeeping and to make possible more accurate cost accounting. The effect, however, has been to make the collective farmer's position more like that of the industrial worker in the city.

The collective-farm system had been devised by Stalin to wean the individual farmer away from his attachment to a given plot of ground by combining his plot with others into a collectively owned unit as distinguished from the state-owned state farms. The latter, while generally more efficient and profitable than collectives, were even less popular because the farmers working them had no title to the soil so dear to every farmer everywhere. An agricultural expert told me that wheat can be grown on state farms at a cost thirty per cent less than on the average collective farm.

I am inclined to believe that Mr. Khrushchev's ultimate objective as indicated by all these reforms is to eliminate gradually all the differences between collective and state farms and eventually to alter the status of the peasant to that of an industrial worker in a factory.

While Khrushchev has introduced badly needed reforms into the Soviet agricultural system and has gone a long way toward solving Russia's food problem, he has thus far failed to demonstrate that the collective system has any inherent advantages over other forms. During a talk with me in the Kremlin, he admitted that the farm problem was far from solved. The collective farmer, he said—unlike the American farmer, who produces primarily to sell his products—is accustomed to producing primarily for his own needs and sells only what is left over. As a consequence, the Soviet collective farm is very wasteful of labor. "Some of our farms," he said frankly, "employ two and three times as much labor as they should. Our chief problem is to change the psychology of our farmers not merely by reorganization but by improving management and leadership. From now on farm management must show more initiative."

Whether he can inspire this new initiative and better management without raising rural living standards far more than he has is not clear. At every farm I visited I asked the question, "What is the average income of a collective farmer?" In every case I was met with evasion either in the form of misleading statistics or by silence. At last I asked a senior official in the Soviet Agricultural Ministry. His answer was equally evasive but more enlightening: "When the time comes we will publish that figure."

Until the Soviet peasant's income has risen from its present unpublishably low level, the Soviet collective-farm system is not likely to attract many imitators.

CHAPTER SEVEN

More Steel

IN SVERDLOVSK I called on the local chairman of the regional economic council, Mr. S. A. Stepanov, and listened to his plans for expanding steel production. He told me that with the new steel they planned not to expand consumer industries but to build machinery for even more steel mills.

"And what are you going to do with that additional steel?" I asked. "Build steel statues?"

"No," he replied solemnly. "More machines for more steel."

The priority on heavy industry which Stalin had decreed still is the law of the land. Back in 1945, when the war was ending, Stalin outlined to me his plans for peacetime industrialization. One of the goals he set was the production of sixty million tons of steel per year. That was more than triple his prewar steel production and five times the then reduced capacity due to war damage. At the time I was very skeptical of the possibility of reaching that goal within the twenty-year time limit set by Stalin. But in 1959, only fourteen years later, steel production will probably reach the sixty-million-ton mark. And further large increases are planned for the coming years.

There can be no doubt that whatever his methods Stalin laid the foundations for Russia's industrial development and prescribed the rules by which they were to be achieved under his direction. While I was in Russia during the war, Stalin's personal supervision not only of the military fronts but of the industrial hinterland was legendary. It was no unusual occurrence for some harried factory manager in the Urals to get a call in the middle of the night from the Kremlin and hear Stalin's angry guttural voice demanding to know why he had fallen behind in the production of rifle barrels or ordering him to step up his output of grenades.

After the war many of his subordinates began to wonder whether this personal supervision and interference were not hindering rather than encouraging greater growth.

"In his later years," Khrushchev told me, "Stalin became distrustful and suspicious. He had a powerful voice which he did not always use in the right way. As he grew older he was unable to direct everything himself but he refused to allow us subordinates to do anything. It was only after his death that we were able to develop initiatives and produce the successes we have today."

The most drastic step toward developing initiatives, as Khrushchev calls it, was taken soon after he reached the pinnnacle of power. He believed that overcentralized control through a maze of ministries and bureaus for almost every branch of industry in Moscow was retarding production. He therefore with one stroke abolished almost all the central ministries and created over a hundred regional economic councils throughout the country to supervise local industrial activities.

While the chairmen of the councils were subordinate to

the central State Planning Commission, they were given wide responsibilities for directing the production and distribution of industrial materials within their jurisdiction.

The innovation was directly contrary to Stalin's principle of stringent supervision from the top, which reflected his own dictatorial and highly suspicious character. Many of Khrushchev's colleagues strongly opposed the decentralization program. (Even Khrushchev has never dared to call it "decentralization.") Some expert foreign observers suspected that Khrushchev was rashly letting go of one of his strongest levers of power by permitting nationalistic authorities in the autonomous republics and provincial authorities in distant areas to direct, even in limited measure, their own economies. Local pride and greed, they predicted, would create little economic autarchies in each area. Regions specializing in certain scarce products would retain those products for their own use and refuse to deliver them to other regions. Thus the monolithic economic structure of the Soviet economy would gradually disintegrate into scores of semi-independent economic states and weaken the Kremlin's control.

These fears and predictions were among the questions I went to the Soviet Union to study. In Moscow I discussed the reorganization with Alexander Kosygin, the head of State Planning, and other central leaders. In every town I visited in the provinces I made a point of calling on the regional chairman. What I found was quite contrary to the prophesies I had heard before. Initiative had been released but central supervision had been retained.

There had, I discovered, been failures of factories in one region to deliver products to factories in other regions, but this had always been true, I was told. While in the old days factories had to route their orders through a series of ministries headed up in Moscow, they are now free to deal directly with their suppliers and to seek supplies from the most economical sources. The head of an auto plant in Moscow told me, for example, that prior to the reforms a plant thousands of miles away at Chelyabinsk in the Urals had been designated by the central ministries to supply him with paint. After the reform he found a factory in Moscow itself which was just as capable of supplying the paint. As a result he was able not only to save on transportation costs but also to cut his inventory of paint supplies in half. Furthermore, he said, if a shipment was below quality he could now take it up directly with the supplier. If the supplier fell behind on deliveries it had to pay him damages amounting to one half of one per cent of the value of the goods for each day's delay.

To an American businessman, Khrushchev's radical reform which caused such concern among his colleagues might appear to be the simplest of common sense. But to Soviet plant managers accustomed to routing their requisitions and sales up through half a dozen bureaus to the central Moscow ministries, and then down again through another half-dozen bureaus to their suppliers or buyers, it has been an almost revolutionary release from bureaucratic chains as well as a source of considerable economies. One Moscow plant manager, for example, told me he had reduced the proportion of out-of-town suppliers of parts and materials from seventy per cent of the total to thirty per cent.

In Kiev I asked the regional economic chairman what happened if his wife demanded some scarce household furniture earmarked by the State Planning authorities for the wife of the chairman of the neighboring economic region. "That," he said with a twinkle, "would depend on my relations with my neighbor's wife." In a more serious vein he went on to explain that the system of penalties laid out in contracts, plus the control and arbitration procedures of the central planners, made it difficult for regions to hoard scarce items destined for other markets.

The new system has encouraged the practice whereby a factory manager urgently in need of certain parts sends a *tolkach* or expediter, to the supplying factory to wangle early delivery, usually by diverting supplies destined for another buyer. A Leningrad factory manager told me that the year before he had frequently resorted to this device though he knew it was against the regulations. However, the central authorities had caught up with him and warned him that in future the salary and the travel expenses of any expediter would be taken from his own salary. He added that now he had to be more careful, as the expenses of one expediter would take most of his salary.

It is, of course, possible that decentralization will in time produce parochial loyalties and tend to fragment the unified Soviet economy, but it seems to me unlikely that such a tendency will become serious in the foreseeable future. In this area as in all others, the Communist Party, whose officials are transferred from one region to another with considerable frequency, is the ardent watchdog.

I was forced to the conclusion, therefore, that Khrushchev's reform has been a powerful stimulant to greater initiative and efficiency and more rational planning, which may well result in a substantial increase in the productivity of Soviet industrial enterprises. But I saw no evidence that for this improvement he had had to pay the price of weakening the Kremlin's control. On the contrary, I found that Khrushchev and his planning officials retained full authority over the economy and that Communist Party officials continue to supervise operations on all levels.

Some people returning from the Soviet Union have reported that the standard of efficiency of Soviet factories is so low that they do not pose a challenge to advanced Western industrial nationals. The ability to build sputniks and nuclear weapons, they argue, represents an advance only on a narrow sector achieved by concentrating all available technical skills on a single point at the expense of the development of other essential sectors of the industrial front. This was another aspect of Soviet heavy industry which I wanted to investigate for myself.

During my visit I looked at a number of automobile and tractor plants, heavy-machinery factories, textile mills, steel mills, hydroelectric stations and coal and iron mines. While the plants I visited were in varying degrees less well laid out, organized and equipped than those in the U.S., my over-all impression was that Soviet factories are producing results despite their lower efficiency. And because of their lower wage rates, their costs may well be below our own.

Another factor in achieving production is the manner in which the goals of the Seven-Year Plan have been brought to each worker. The national target has been broken down not only to each factory but to each shop in each factory. Every week each workman knows whether his own group is ahead of or behind its quota in the great national objective. I was struck by the interest and pride I found on the part of individual workers in their own contribution to the national goal. This system has been worked out with meticulous care by Moscow. Chief Planner Kosygin told me in explanation, "When fifty million workers agree on one plan it works."

"Catch up with and surpass America" is a slogan used everywhere in Russia to encourage hard work and to justify present-day sacrifices.

One of the weaknesses of the Soviet planned economy is its emphasis on numbers and the reward system based on quantity of production. Khrushchev himself complained to me of the tendency of Soviet factory managers to concentrate production on items that could be turned out rapidly rather than on those requiring more time and effort.

During my visit to Russia in 1941 to negotiate an aid agreement with Stalin, I had seen entire factories being evacuated from Moscow, which was then threatened by the Germans. Stalin told me that when plants were moved behind the Urals the factory workers rode on the same train with the machinery and equipment. Later these same plants were put into operation again and the tanks and equipment they turned out made a substantial contribution to the Russian war effort.

I recently visited one of these plants in Sverdlovsk. In fact, its director and several of its engineers who had been evacuated in 1941 from Leningrad gave me a dinner in a tent pitched by the side of the marker in the Ural mountains dividing Europe from Asia. They described to me how they had set up their shops in the open air and had managed to get roofs over them only a few days before the first winter snows fell. They told me that they had also converted their operations from the manufacture of electrical equipment to that of fuses. Not until the war ended did they go back to their original task of making switches and generators. The example of these evacuated plants demonstrated to me that even under primitive conditions and with unsuitable equipment, the capacity of Soviet engineers for improvisation is remarkable.

In Stalingrad I visited a tractor plant that had been completely destroyed during the great battle for that city, except for its power plant, which supplied electricity for a large area between the lines. Several times the power plant changed hands, but during the entire siege it remained in operation, sometimes under German control, sometimes under Soviet, because the electricity it furnished was essential to both camps.

Rebuilt, the tractor plant now employs sixteen thousand workers, who turn out one hundred large tractors a day. It was raining when I visited the assembly shop, and the steel floors were dirty and slick. The roof was leaking and at one point I saw a young girl operating a heavy machine tool while a steady steam of water fell on her kerchiefed head. The plant's chief engineer hustled me on, but not before the girl had given me a somewhat watery grin.

As in every plant I visited, the workers were curious and friendly and crowded around me to ask questions. It was therefore difficult to reach any judgment about the speed or the effectiveness of their operations. However, it seemed to me that both the housekeeping and the layout were somewhat primitive. Perhaps this was why the chief engineer told me he had no plan of the plant when I asked to see one.

At the auto works in Moscow, formerly called the Stalin Plant (until Stalin's down grading), there was better organization and the assembly line seemed to operate more smoothly and rationally. Here again I was constantly surrounded by workers. One of them, a young girl, told me she remembered me from war days when I went for walks with my daughter in the Arbat district, where she lived. A few workers were less friendly and asked heckling questions, obviously on orders. They were easy to spot from the self-conscious swagger they adopted to conceal their nervousness when they approached. Almost invariably they launched into a tirade denouncing American warmongers or asking angrily why we rejected Nikita Sergeevich's (Khrushchev's) proposals for arms limitations.

The Soviet automobile industry has been modeled from the start on the American example. The first Soviet plant at Gorki was designed, built and put into operation by Ford engineers. Every new Soviet model since has been copied from an American prototype. In my talks with Deputy Premier Kozlov I expressed the view that American manufacturers had concentrated too heavily on large cars, and he admitted quite frankly that the Soviet engineers had followed this bad example. He hoped that in the future they would turn out smaller cars, he said. The Seven-Year Plan contemplates no great expansion in cars, and the production of small cars apparently is being postponed for another decade or more.

Current production of motor vehicles is at the rate of about half a million a year, of which only 120,000 are passenger cars—mostly for official use. At the end of the Seven-Year Plan, about 850,000 vehicles, chiefly trucks and buses, are to be produced. Only 150,000 will be cars—hardly more than at present. Thus by 1965 the U.S.S.R. will have only about one and a half per cent of the cars we have on the road in 1959.

From what I learned of the Soviet plans for car production, I doubt whether Soviet leaders ever contemplate mass production on our scale. "We do not plan to provide everyone with a car," one official told me. "We will devote our energies to developing better mass transportation than you have." However, the craving I found among all the people I met for a private car may create pressures which the leaders will find difficult to ignore completely.

The history of the Soviet car industry illustrates another significant feature of Soviet designing—the tendency of engineers in consumer industries to follow closely the example of the most advanced industries abroad rather than strike out for themselves with new designs to meet their special situations.

At Timur Tao near Karaganda in central Kazakhstan I was shown a steel mill rising out of the arid steppe. Beside it construction gangs were building a town for its future workers—using Mr. Khrushchev's concrete methods. The mill itself was obviously of modern design and the workmanship going into its construction was clearly of high order. The director, an engineer with long experience in the construction of steel plants, told me he had been earmarked to supervise the building of the Soviet-financed steel mill at Bhilai in India (which I had previously visited) but had managed to wangle his way out of the assignment. "India is too hot," he explained. The Timur Tao mill will begin to produce steel ingots in 1959 and when finally completed will have a capacity of over three million tons of rolled steel plate.

One of the most impressive industrial enterprises I saw in the Soviet Union was the opencast iron mine of Rudni in northern Kazakhstan. In 1948 an airplane pilot attached to a prospecting party exploring a neighboring area had noted that his special electromagnetic-photo prospecting equipment reacted violently every time he flew over an area containing a pig farm in the desert north of the town of Kustanai. Scientists concluded that there must be iron deposits in the area. After making borings they found they had hit upon one of the largest iron ore deposits ever discovered in the Soviet Union, with now proven reserves of a billion and a half tons of high-grade iron ore so close to the surface that it could be extracted by opencast methods.

In 1955 excavating operations were begun, over the angry protests of the local pig farmers. (I was surprised to learn that pig farmers are allowed to raise their voices in the Soviet Union, until it was explained that it was a state pig farm.) When I arrived excavators had already dug a giant pit in the overburden of clay and gravel a hundred and fifty feet deep and several miles long and the first iron ore was being extracted. When both pits are in full operation a few years hence, they will be producing over twenty million tons of ore each year.

As I watched from the lip of the chasm, the director of the mine unrolled maps and charts and described in detail the size and shape of the deposits and the methods being used to extract the ore. It occurred to me that during Stalin's lifetime the information he was giving me would have been considered top secret, but today Khrushchev and his subordinates are so self-confident that they are eager to divulge the extent of their resources.

Giant excavators with a capacity up to fifteen cubic yards were being used to remove the overburden. A fleet of 25-ton and 10-ton dump trucks were driving at high speeds up and down well-surfaced roads at regular intervals while sprinklers watered the lanes to keep down the dust. An electric railroad along the side of the cut was also removing the waste and dumping it a mile or more away. At the bottom of the pit we watched miners blasting the heavy red ore and loading it into trucks to be taken to nearby crushers, whence it was transported to steel mills in Chelyabinsk in the Ural area to the north. Development work, I was told, is starting in two other similar deposits about fifty miles away. According to plan, when these are in operation the area will produce up to eighty-three million tons of ore a year.

For some years a major theme of Russian propaganda has been the gigantic earth-moving operations the Soviets are undertaking in the Siberian wastes. Mountains to be tunneled, rivers to be dammed and reversed to flow into the Asian desert instead of the Arctic Sea, and other equally sensational undertakings are projected. When I arrived in Moscow and asked to see one of these projects, I was told they were all in the planning stage. "Siberia is still just a great big empty place," a high official told me.

I had all but abandoned the idea when I read in the newspapers that Mr. Khrushchev had noted in a speech that I wanted to go to the great new hydroelectric project at Bratsk north of Lake Baikal. "We know Mr. Harriman from the days when he was ambassador during the war. Since then he has made several anti-Soviet speeches. But if he wants to see Bratsk let him go and see how the great Soviet people are making miracles in the primeval taiga."

As a result of these comments, at the end of my tour I found myself on a jet airliner bound for Irkutsk near Lake Baikal. It was a 3,000-mile journey and took some eight hours. From Irkutsk I transferred to a smaller plane and flew north into the wilderness, landing on a dirt strip in the middle of the Siberian forests. My coming must have been publicized, for a considerable crowd was waiting at the airport and cheered as I stepped from the plane. After a long drive along a dirt road through the wilderness, I reached the dam site.

Another crowd of several thousand greeted me with cheers at the dam and thronged around me to shake hands with the first American ever to have seen the project. The construction chief announced to me that the last gap in the dam was being closed that very day. As we watched from the operations tower overlooking the site, a fleet of trucks dumped the last loads of rock and gravel into the gap. While the crowds cheered and a band blared, the Angara River, which once rushed past at the rate of three thousand cubic yards per second, was brought under control.

The dam site itself, between two granite cliffs, is an engineer's dream. When the dam is finally completed two years hence, it will rise nearly four hundred feet above the river bed. The reservoir it will create will extend up the river 350 miles and contain 145 million acre-feet of water —more than forty times as much as our largest reservoir at Hoover Dam. Already the hundred thousand people from collective-farm villages in the area to be flooded are being moved to new lands which are being cleared from the Siberian jungle, where they will be compensated acre for acre and house for house for their condemned farms.

The generator plant to be erected at the site will have a capacity of more than twice that of Grand Coulee, the largest in America, and is planned to produce over four million kilowatts of firm power. The Angara is the only outlet of Lake Baikal, which itself drains over four hundred smaller rivers and acts as a natural reservoir, thus assuring a stable minimum flow. As a result of this unusually steady flow, the electricity produced with it will be the cheapest in all the Soviet Union.

I asked what use could be made of such immense quantities of power in this remote wilderness, and the construction chief explained that a number of factories for pulp, cellulose and synthetic fibers would be built in the vicinity. I also learned that an aluminum plant will be built to exploit local bauxite deposits. The construction chief explained that a 300-mile power line will carry the power to the eastern Siberian grid, which connects with such distant places as Vladivostok on the Pacific coast.

Previously experts in high-tension transmission lines at Leningrad and Sverdlovsk had explained to me that the Bratsk power line would operate at five hundred thousand volts—considerably higher than any in the United States—thus reducing transmission losses. They also told me, incidentally, that they were making large-scale experiments in transmitting power by direct rather than alternating current in order to reduce transmission losses still further. They added that there is presently a considerable debate going on between advocates of alternating current and those of direct current. It is, I imagine, one of the few debates sufficiently remote from ideological doctrine to be discussed in freedom within the Soviet Union. Prior to my visit to Bratsk, I had seen another great hydroelectric plant, on the Volga at Stalingrad. It will product 2.3 million kilowatts. During my talks with Mr. Kosygin of the State Planning Commission in Moscow I had raised the question whether they included interest on the large investments in these projects when computing the cost of power. The interpreter, however, had great difficulty finding language to translate my meaning, apparently because Karl Marx had denounced interest as an evil device of capitalists. So I asked Mr. Kosygin in a different way: "How does the Soviet government measure the relative value of capital investments in reckoning the cost of one of these gigantic plants?" Kosygin acknowledged that in recent years Soviet economists had been having difficulties with this problem. They had solved it, he said, by reckoning the number of years a capital investment needed to pay for itself. He called it "the rate of capital turnover." From other Soviet economists I learned that they find the device a cumbersome one, and some even predict that within a few years they will have to abandon pretense and acknowledge that, despite Marx, interest is an essential element of modern economy, whether Communist or capitalist.

Mr. Kosygin had also told me that the high initial investment costs of some hydroelectric projects in comparison with thermal stations indicated that the Soviet Union had gone about as far in this direction as they considered advisable. From now on, he said, they planned to maintain the existing ratio between water and thermal power, i.e., about twenty to eighty. This, he pointed out, was approximately the same as the ratio in the United States, indicating that in this respect too the problems of a Communist economy were not so different from those of capitalism. From other sources I learned that the proportion of hydroelectric plants will even be reduced in the future partly because of the discovery of natural-gas deposits for fuel for thermal plants.

Those whose study of geography ended as late as ten years ago will find that their concept of the natural resources of the Soviet Union requires considerable revision. Stalin had laid great stress on the necessity for exploring the relatively unknown areas of Siberia and Kazakhstan for mineral deposits, and as early as the thirties he was pressing the study of geology. Since the war, these measures have been paying off at a remarkable rate. Even in Czarist times it was known that the mineral wealth of the Urals was unusually great though it had never been systematically explored. Today it is a favorite and common boast of geologists in Asiatic Russia that the Kazakh steppes and Siberia have been found to contain all the elements in the universe. At Sverdlovsk I was taken through a geological museum which is said to be unique for its exhibits of rare metals and ores, all of which have been found in the surrounding areas. Whether or not the claim is accurate, I do not recall ever having seen such a variety of geological specimens collected from one area.

As a result of the activities of Soviet geologists in the past ten years, not only have great deposits of iron ore such as those at Rudni been unearthed but many other rare and useful elements have been located. In the Don Basin large deposits of natural gas have been opened up and already many cities of central Russia are connected with the field by pipelines. In another year Leningrad too will be supplied with natural gas. Another deposit has been discovered more recently in the neighborhood of Bokhara in Central Asia, once famous only for its rugs. Plans are being made to pipe the gas up north to the new industrial area of central Siberia.

Another reward of the early priority given by Stalin to the study of geology has been the great advance in new techniques of prospecting. "Our old methods have permitted us to discover only what is immediately below the earth's surface," a leading geologist, Mr. K. M. Abdulaev, president of the Uzbek Academy of Sciences, told me. "Now we must devise new methods to explore resources lying far below the surface."

Already, he explained, the new techniques have disclosed rich deposits hidden from less advanced prospecting. Electromagnetic photography and water analysis have, for example, yielded rich results.

According to another concept widespread in the United States and other Western countries, the Soviet Union is seriously lacking one essential resourse—manpower. As a result of the sharp decline in the birth rate during the war years, the generation now entering the factories is much smaller than normal. Many of Khrushchev's current reforms, including the educational reforms, are ascribed to this shortage.

This, of course, was one of the theories I looked into

with special care during my visit. Factory managers told me that they did have some trouble getting skilled workers, and in Leningrad Mayor Smirnov said that if they could satisfy ninety-five per cent of the demands of plant managers for labor they considered it normal. However, in no case did I find any sense of urgency or alarm among the managers about this shortage, and I had the impression that their concern was not appreciably greater than the normal complaining of businessmen anywhere about the scarcity of skilled labor.

I also discussed the problem with several of the top Soviet leaders, including Mr. Khrushchev. He told me that the youngest generation of workers was indeed considerably smaller than in the past. However, he said, this is not the problem it might seem to be. The trouble with the Soviet economy, he said quite frankly, was its inefficiency and low productivity. This was the problem which was of greatest concern to the Kremlin. If the existing labor force could come somewhat closer to the productivity of American labor, he indicated, the decline of manpower would be no problem.

He stated, for example, that the plenary meeting of the Central Committee of the Communist Party scheduled to open the day after our first talk was concentrating on pushing measures for rationalizing working methods, modernizing plant equipment and developing automation.

Of course, he added, the need for increased manpower as a result of the industrial expansion envisaged in the Seven-Year Plan could not be met entirely by this method. As new industries are created, new sources of manpower must be found. But, he added, the Soviet Union has a potential surplus of manpower on the farms. As I have already noted, he said that some farms now employ two and three times too many workers. With better management and more machinery adaquate manpower could be made available when and if needed from the villages.

Some Americans have suggested that Khrushchev's reliance on the rural labor reserve is illusory. How, they ask, are you going to lure the peasant from his land? I do not believe that the Soviet Union will have any more trouble getting peasants to the city than other countries have experienced in the course of their industrialization—and probably a good deal less. For many years strict police measures forbidding nonresidents to move into the larger cities have had to be taken to prevent an excess flow from the farms. Mr. Khrushchev believes that as he needs industrial labor the efficiency of the collective farms will have increased sufficiently to release the workers he requires. I suspect that many peasants are only too eager to give up their primitive existence on collective farms for the less monotonous life of the city.

There will, of course, be some areas where it will be more difficult to attract skilled labor than in others. At Bratsk in Siberia, for example, I found wage rates for construction labor were almost double those in European Russian cities. It will also take time to educate the peasant population for factory jobs. However, this has been a problem faced by every country in the process of industrialization and one in which the Soviets have had much experience in the past two decades. Indeed, the widespread educational system makes it probably easier for them to solve this problem than for many countries which built factories before they provided mass education.

If further evidence is needed that the manpower shortage is not a serious problem it can be found in the current reduction in working hours from forty-six to forty-one hours per week in most heavy industries. Wherever I went I asked economists and factory managers why they had chosen the start of the grandiose Seven-Year Plan to reduce working hours. Some replied that the Twenty-first Party Congress had promised this reduction to the workers and that the congress' promises must be honored. One reason for the congress' solicitude no doubt was a genuine desire to relieve some of the pressures—particularly in the case of women—under which the Soviet people have been working since the start of the regime. No doubt, too, the value of the move to Soviet propaganda abroad was not overlooked.

I was also told that the loss of man-hours would be almost completely compensated for by "more rational" organization and better machinery. While they denied that this meant raising work norms and insisted that, in contrast to the practice under Stalin, current regulations forbid raising norms without providing more efficient machinery of labor-saving devices, I had the strong impression that they were counting on a speed-up of production per hour. At all events, I was surprised to find the extent to which both factory managers and political leaders talked about production costs and profits.

Although I have no way of knowing whether they will achieve the ambitious goals of the Seven-Year Plan, I came away from the Soviet Union with little evidence of insuperable difficulties in the future industrial expansion of the country. Though many of their factories are inefficient, the Russians are masters of improvisation. In some fields I found their technology as good as if not (as in the case of high-tension transmission) better than our own. In natural resources I did not see any evidence of serious bottlenecks— not even, as yet, in manpower.

CHAPTER EIGHT

Terror

THROUGHOUT THEIR LONG HISTORY the Russian people have feared the Kremlin and the Kremlin has feared the people.

Since I was last in Russia great changes have been reported on the part terror plays in the Soviet Union. This, of course, was one of the major questions I came to examine. What I saw gave me some real encouragement.

There is no doubt that while Stalin lived the Russian people were ruled largely by fear. By nature a morbid and suspicious character, he became almost pathologically afraid after his friend Sergei Kirov was assassinated in Leningrad in 1934. He seldom ventured from the Kremlin, whose gates were guarded by cordons of soldiers and secret police, and when he did he traveled in a cortege of fast limousines, their windows bulletproofed and their curtains drawn.

The purges that began with Kirov's death and reached their height in the late thirties provoked an equal fear on the part of the people for the tyrant. It is estimated that tens of thousands were shot and millions sent off to the Far North and Siberia to work the lumber camps and mines.

Even in the war the terror continued, for Stalin's military

police who watched over the loyalty of the Soviet soldiers treated capture as sabotage and retreat as treason. Once during the war when I was praising the bravery of the Russian troops during an engagement in which they had pressed forward under withering German fire, Stalin replied cryptically, "In the Soviet Army it takes more courage to retreat than to advance."

After the war, as Khrushchev revealed in his famous secret speech at the Twentieth Party Congress, Stalin became even more capricious. His closest subordinates in the Kremlin had no security. Quoting Bulganin, Khrushchev said, "It has happened sometimes that one goes to Stalin on his invitation as a friend and when one sits down with him one doesn't know where one will be sent next—home or to jail."

The so-called "doctors' plot," in which a number of doctors were accused of conspiring to assassinate some leading Communists, was apparently concocted by Stalin to launch another purge, and some foreign observers of Russia have suggested that the men around him, fearful of losing their own lives in another mass terror, murdered the old man himself. I have always questioned this. During one of my long talks with Khrushchev recently, he revealed his version of Stalin's death. Later, at my request, he gave me permission to publish it.

Stalin, Khrushchev told me, had become far more suspicious, arbitrary and ruthless in his later years than when I had known him during the war. "He trusted no one and none of us could trust him. He would not let us do the work he was no longer capable of. It was very difficult for us.

"One Saturday night he invited us all to his *dacha* in the country for dinner," he went on. "Stalin was in a good humor. It was a gay evening and we all had a good time.

Then we went home. On Sundays Stalin usually telephoned each of us to discuss business, but that Sunday he did not call, which struck us as odd. He did not come back to town on Monday, and on Monday evening the head of his bodyguard called us and said Stalin was ill.

"All of us—Beria, Malenkov, Bulganin and I—hurried out to the country to see him. He was already unconscious. A blood clot had paralyzed an arm, a leg and his tongue. We stayed with him for three days but he remained unconscious. Then for a time he came out of his coma and we went into his room. A nurse was feeding him tea with a spoon. He shook us by the hand and tried to joke with us, smiling feebly and waving with his good arm to a picture over his bed of a baby lamb being fed with a spoon by a little girl. Now, he indicated by gestures, he was just as helpless as the baby lamb.

"Some time later he died," Khrushchev continued. "I wept. After all, we were all his pupils and owed him everything. Like Peter the Great, Stalin fought barbarism with barbarism but he was a great man."

The barbaric terror Stalin had created did not end with his death. I asked whether Stalin had selected a successor before he died. Almost bitterly Khrushchev replied, "He chose no one. He thought he would live forever." The little band he left leaderless must have looked fearfully at each other, silently posing Lenin's old question, "Who—whom?" Unable to select one head, they formed shifting cliques and alliances, carefully maneuvering so that no single one gained absolute control.

Beria, the chief of the police, was a special problem. Heading the whole vast police network, he might, if he dared, seize power for himself. Whether he actually tried we do not know. Khrushchev has told me, however, that

Beria was not only a rascal but "an adventurer" as well—
indicating that Beria had actually entertained ideas of an
adventurous attempt to seize power.

So Beria was seized and held for months in prison.
Finally, because there was no place in the Soviet Union
safe enough to contain him, they shot him, just as Stalin
had taught them to shoot anyone they could not absolutely
trust.

Those who survived Beria could not agree on a basic
policy. Occasionally some seem to have advocated a re-
versal of Stalin's policy of fear and a relaxation of the grip
in which the police held the people. Others apparently believed that survival could be won only by sticking to the
one policy they knew—Stalin's terror.

Soon afterward a group of them proposed that the Kremlin, the grim symbol of tyranny, should be opened to the
public. Molotov and others, Mikoyan told me, strongly
opposed this innovation. "But," Mikoyan said with a confident smile, "it was only the first time Molotov found
himself outvoted." The Kremlin was opened. When I had
first entered it to see Stalin on a dark and rainy night in
1941, my car was stopped as we entered the forbidding
gates and several policemen carefully scrutinized it. Before
I reached Stalin's office I had to pass several more police
cordons. But now when I visited it, children were playing
in the gardens while their parents sunned themselves and
tourists wandered casually among the museums and
churches within the walls.

Gradually a real change had come over Stalin's successors. Now, with Beria gone, no single man had the
power of life over the others and they apparently decided
that to continue the terror would be suicidal. Not only did
they stop shooting each other but they stopped sending each

other to prison. They could still send each other to minor jobs far from Moscow, as they sent Molotov to Mongolia and Malenkov to Kazakhstan, but this was hardly to be compared with brutal exile to labor camps.

Gradually too the decision-making group was broadened. When Khrushchev appealed to the hundred-man Central Committee after he had been overruled by Molotov and his colleagues in the Presidium, he established a precedent that may have far-reaching importance. For he and his successors may find it difficult to rule in the future without a majority of the Central Committee on their side.

But one problem they have not solved is that of succession. Khrushchev complained to me that Stalin had appointed no successor, and he indicated that he would not repeat the error. Turning to Mikoyan, he added, "'That's a mistake Anastas and I have agreed won't be made again." However, I wonder whether when he dies those in the leadership who remain will readily acquiesce to his selection of an heir apparent.

The change of attitude among the Kremlin rivals was made very clear to us during our talks in the Kremlin. Beria, of course, was dismissed as a scoundrel and an adventurer. Malenkov, Khrushchev said, was a loyal worker as long as he was a subordinate. "He wrote a fine speech for others, but he could never decide what he himself should say. When he took command he was no good at all," Khrushchev concluded contemptuously.

Khrushchev's attitude toward Molotov was something quite different. "We must respect Molotov," he said to me. "He has firm convictions and he sticks to them, though I often disagree with them." Mikoyan added, "Molotov has fine qualities but he is too set in his views. He cannot accept new approaches to problems." It is hard to imagine

Stalin being as generous with even the most insignificant of his alleged opponents.

When I was having dinner with Mr. Khrushchev and his two deputies, Mikoyan and Kozlov, Khrushchev started to complain jokingly about Mikoyan's failings. I said I had found him one of the toughest traders during my negotiations in Moscow during the war. I suggested he would have been a great capitalist and would have amassed a large fortune and become one of the most successful exploiters of labor. Khrushchev agreed. "I've always said Mikoyan was born a generation too late," he said.

I said that it was not too late and that if he ever tired of Mikoyan he should send him to America and not to Siberia. Mikoyan broke in: "Nikita can't send me to Siberia any more. He's too late. That sort of thing is ended."

I thought back to the days when I had been with Stalin in similar company. Would any of them have dared question Stalin's powers of life and death even in the wildest jest?

Perhaps more important than the truce they concluded among themselves was the decision to extend it to the people, who had lived with terror since the Revolution. They realized that without Stalin's prestige and the awful fear he could inspire, rule by terror would be difficult if not impossible. They realized too that the Soviet people were tired to death of the grueling conditions under which they worked.

They also made the interesting discovery that the slave labor camps where prisoners worked without pay were actually highly uneconomical. Therefore as soon as Beria was disposed of they put the police under not a single man but a committee and immediately began to curtail its powers. No longer was it legal to knock on a door at midnight and take someone off to prison without trial or investigation. The Draconian labor laws Stalin had decreed during the war were formally taken off the books, and the gigantic slave labor camps that scarred the countryside were gradually reduced in size. Some of the inmates were turned free, others "induced" to remain and work as free laborers in the areas where they had been confined.

I had carefully followed all these changes since Stalin's death, but I was anxious to see for myself just how far they had gone. When I came to Moscow I asked, among other things, to visit one of the new prison work camps in Siberia which had been reformed. Mikoyan told me there was no such thing as a prison camp anymore. They had all been abolished. But the very next day Khrushchev, who was on a speaking tour, referred to my request and said, "Let Mr. Harriman go to Siberia. The bourgeois press is shouting that the country is being built up by people in [prison] camps. Of course there still are people in prisons in the U.S.S.R. paying the penalty for crimes and thievery, but no one wants them for construction work as their productivity is so low since they are working not voluntarily but by compulsion."

A few hours later a "correction colony" was added to my itinerary. It was about forty miles from Moscow and was rated by the prison director as a "general-regimen" or average prison.

The Klyukova prison contained about a thousand inmates serving from one to ten years. The majority were employed in the prison workshops making aluminum pots, pans and other articles, including firemen's helmets. For this they were paid a small wage—about half the standard scale—which, after deductions for food and clothing, they could either spend in the prison canteen or send to their families.

The prison itself was surrounded by a high wooden fence

topped with barbed wire and with watchtowers at frequent intervals. Inside this enclosure were the administration buildings, the foundry, the workshops and the prison garden. In the center was a second enclosure surrounded by another wooden wall in which the prisoners were kept when not at work. Here we saw their dormitories, where they slept eight to forty in a room on narrow, double-decker iron cots. Here, too, was their mess hall, a library, a "club" with a stage and an auditorium for several hundred, and their playing fields, where some of them were playing basketball, volleyball and ping-pong.

The Soviet Ministry of Education maintains at the prison a school with twelve teachers where about a quarter of the inmates study. They may either take regular courses in the ten-year Soviet school curriculum or take special courses to qualify them as skilled tractor drivers, electricians or mechanics.

Most of the prisoners, according to the prison director, had been convicted of theft or "hooliganism"—the Soviet term for rowdyism, which usually involves disturbing the peace or rioting under the influence of liquor. For good behavior sentences can be reduced by half. For bad behavior prisoners can be committed to up to five days' solitary confinement or in extreme cases transferred to strict security prisons where, I gathered, the regimen is far more severe.

Prisoners have the right to correspond with their families and to see them periodically. One unusual feature of the camp was a provision for week-long visits by wives and children two or three times a year. For this purpose a number of small rooms have been put aside outside the inner enclosure where visiting wives can live with inmates. Explaining this procedure, the prison director stated that one of the most serious problems of prison terms was the effect on families. The provision for week-long visits was an attempt to preserve the family unity during the prison term. In view of the early Marxist belief that the family is a decadent remnant of "bourgeois" prejudice, I was impressed by the Soviet penologists' solicitude for its preservation.

On the whole I was also impressed by the sensible attitude of the prison staff toward their problems. I was not, however, entirely surprised. In the early days of the Communist regime, in fact until Stalin's extreme terror started in the early thirties, the Soviets had prided themselves on their progressive prison system, which, they maintained, was directed not toward punishment but toward correction. The new look of today in Soviet prisons therefore is not as new as it might seem, but rather a reversion to the Leninist period.

It has been suggested that Klyukova prison is a "show prison" maintained to show foreigners. When I went there I was the second American to have been allowed inside. (Subsequently a group of visiting American governors were taken to it.) I rather doubt, therefore, that it is a show place. It takes a fertile imagination to believe that Khrushchev, with his practical and highly cost-conscious mind, would keep a thousand men in jail for years on end for the edification of a handful of foreigners. Doubtless it was one of the better prison establishments. In fact, its officials stated quite freely that other prisons exist for more serious offenders where the regimen is much more severe.

Throughout my travels in Siberia and other outlying places I saw no traces of large prison camps. This of course does not necessarily mean they do not exist. Though the Soviet authorities state that there are no more "political prisoners," political opposition is a crime and political treason is one of the few offenses for which the death penalty still exists in the Soviet Union. However, there are certainly no longer the mass arrests that there were under Stalin.

Under Stalin Karaganda had been notorious for the huge prison colonies which worked its coal mines, and in his day foreigners were never allowed to visit it. In fact, I was told I was the first American visitor. I motored about the town and its environs for a great many miles and saw one of the old stockades still standing. Its watchtowers were unmanned and the area inside was being broken up for a workers' housing development.

The chairman of the regional economic council told me that prison labor in the mines had been abolished in 1954—the year after Stalin's death. Repeating Mr. Khrushchev's explanation, he said they had found that prisoners were not mining enough coal to make it worth while. It has been estimated that many tens of thousands of prisoners worked the mines during the Stalin period. In 1945, when coal was desperately needed, they mined only twelve million tons. Today twenty-four thousand free miners are employed in the shafts and turn out twenty-three million tons in a year.

The effect of Khrushchev's easing of Stalin's terror struck me even before I crossed the Soviet frontier. In the Soviet jet in which I traveled from Paris another passenger introduced himself, saying he remembered me from war days, when his ministry had dealt with me. At that time he had been a transportation engineer. Now he was Deputy Minister of Railroads. Quite freely he discussed current Soviet transportation problems and practices and cited statistics, facts and plans which in Stalin's time no Soviet official would have dared discuss with a foreigner. The very fact that he had approached me with such freedom illustrated the new atmosphere prevailing in the Soviet Union toward foreigners.

It would, of course, be a mistake to overestimate the extent of this changed attitude. The Russians for centuries have been fearful of foreigners and xenophobic in their treatment of them. Peter the Great, who had "opened a window to Europe" and welcomed foreigners, nevertheless confined them to a sort of ghetto in Moscow which only privileged officials were permitted to enter. He himself was a constant visitor there.

As late as the nineteenth century and right up to the first war, foreigners were generally kept under strict police surveillance and even those families of foreign merchants who had lived for generations in Russia did not mingle in Russian society or welcome Russians to mingle in theirs.

The situation is not far different today. The facts that few Russians have apartments adequate for entertainment and that the Soviet officials are reluctant to have foreigners see in what poor housing conditions the average Soviet citizen lives operate as effective restraints against excessive familiarity with foreigners. When I was in Moscow during the war a number of Russians were permitted to come to the embassy and a few even entertained me in their apartments. But following the war, shortly after I left, the bars came down again and Russians who had been friends with foreigners when we were allied in the war now shunned them coldly and crossed the street to avoid facing a former acquaintance. Today the situation has changed again. Visitors are greeted with great friendliness in public places, though I doubt whether many visit private homes or form permanent friendships.

It would be illusory to expect this centuries-old Russian

reluctance to fraternize with foreigners as in Western countries to vanish overnight, and I am sure that Mr. Khrushchev has no intention of permitting it to occur. Nevertheless, the innate hospitality of the Russian, combined with a passionate curiosity about the outside world, especially among the educated Soviet youth, is creating strong pressures against the barrier. Furthermore, the very fact that Mr. Khrushchev is holding up life in the United States as a model for the Soviet Union to catch up with is creating a genuine admiration for Americans.

Before I met Mr. Khrushchev a highly placed friend of his said to me privately, "Stalin was like what his name implies in Russian—a man of steel. To convert Russia from a backward rural community into an industrial power he spared neither himself nor the people. In that he was like Peter the Great, whom he often talked about. His approach was impersonal and his decisions were governed by a code of laws and rules which he himself devised and enforced.

"Khrushchev is a man of another epoch," he went on. "The Soviet Union no longer needs to suffer and sacrifice as it did in the first stages of industrialization. You have just seen for yourself that life in the new frontier towns of Kazakhstan is not as rugged as it was in Moscow when you first visited in 1926.

"Khrushchev has roots that go deep into the soil. He has a strong feeling for people and his approach to problems is personal and practical."

The difference between Stalin and Khrushchev emerged the moment I met the latter. He received me in Stalin's old office in the Kremlin and I noticed that it seemed bigger. Khrushchev explained that he had enlarged it by adding a small room Stalin had used as a rest room. Khrushchev apparently finds no need to take naps while he works. The long table we sat at was the same as the one Stalin had had, but Khrushchev had moved it from the inner wall of the office to the window side, where the outside world sheds more light upon it. The same pictures of Marx and Lenin hung on the wall, but Khrushchev had added a third— an oil painting of a hydroelectric plant built since Stalin died.

On a small table was a glittering model of a Soviet tank, which he showed me. "Some Americans who saw it said later that Khrushchev has a golden tank on his desk," he said. "Actually it is brass and was given me by the officers of the Soviet Army stationed in Germany. Although I had to accept it in order not to hurt their feelings, I told them never to give me presents like that again."

Publicly Stalin had permitted the most abject adulation of himself and accepted without hesitation every tribute and gift offered him, believing it was good propaganda. But privately he combined great dignity with an almost unpretentious modesty. In 1942 when I accompanied Churchill to Moscow to see him, we found him wearing for the first time the uniform of Marshal of the Soviet Union, a title he had just assumed. Churchill admired the uniform and congratulated Stalin on his elevation, but Stalin brushed the compliment aside with an unassuming manner. "They said I ought to accept the position of head of the armed forces in order to improve the morale of the troops," he said modestly. Just who "they" were was not made clear.

Toward his subordinates Stalin was ruthless, overbearing and coldly impersonal. On one occasion I urged him to send Molotov, then his Foreign Minister, to the first United Nations conference in San Francisco. Molotov had objected strenuously on the ground that he was too busy. "I haven't the time, time, time," he kept repeating. But Stalin imperiously rejected his objections. Ignoring his Foreign Minister, he turned to me and said, "He will go." And needless to say he went.

Khrushchev is much more personal, though no more considerate of his associates. During one of our talks in the presence of Gromyko, his Foreign Minister, he said, "Gromyko says only what we tell him to. If he doesn't we'll fire him and get someone who does." Gromyko, sitting across the table, looked glummer than ever.

Toward children Stalin had a genuine warmth, I think, and he was often photographed with them. When General Eisenhower visited Moscow after the war in July 1945 Stalin invited us both to review the great Youth Parade from the parapet over Lenin's tomb. A man in the parade brought a child up to Stalin, who swept his arm around her affectionately. She snuggled up to him, delighted, feeling, I am sure, far more secure than he ever did despite the cordon of police who always surrounded him.

Khrushchev too can be affectionate and he spoke often of his grandson. When we were taking a walk in the country we found a hedgehog in the woods. Gingerly but expertly Khrushchev picked it up and gave it to one of his guards with careful instructions to put it in a box with straw and send it to the boy. When I saw him next I asked him how his grandson had liked his new pet. "He never even saw it," Khrushchev said dejectedly. "His mother objected too much. I have had the guard take it back to the woods where we found it and let it go."

Although Stalin's propaganda machine spared no pains to portray him as the revered and beloved father of his people, I never had the impression he relished associating with them. He was often photographed in cozy chats with workmen and peasants, but he seldom appeared in public and hardly ever made speeches even over the radio.

Khrushchev, on the other hand, seems to seek personal popularity in the same way as grass-roots politicians, by mingling with people. He is forever traveling about the country addressing crowds of peasants and working people in lengthy speeches filled with personal appeals and often so earthy that they must be carefully edited before they are printed. These barnstorming tours are more than political propaganda campaigns. They reflect a personal urge to be liked, and, though he has not won the deep respect tinged with fear which the Soviet people acquired for Stalin as a war leader, he has, I believe, gained a degree of popular affection at least among the peasantry and the working people.

Stalin ruled by fear and was ruled by it. Khrushchev has sought to lessen the fear and to rule as much as possible by persuasion. Nor does he himself seem to have fear.

After our meeting in Stalin's room in the Kremlin we talked for an hour or more and then Khrushchev suggested we go to the country for dinner. With interpreters and aides we were five, more than could be seated in the rear of his big limousine. So Khrushchev turned to his bodyguard, who was sitting beside the chauffeur, and told him to make room for one of the party. "I feel perfectly safe traveling with an American," he said, laughing.

Carefully the chauffeur drove the car across the Kremlin square, where Soviet tourists and holidaymakers were casually jaywalking, and passed through the once heavily guarded Kremlin gate. We drove through town at a reasonable pace, slowing down occasionally with the traffic. There was none of the frenzied speed which Stalin had insisted on.

No blinds were drawn. No car full of armed guards preceded us, and behind us came only one other car carrying the bodyguard. The Kremlin, I thought, no longer fears the people.

As we drove through the countryside Khrushchev talked about the meeting of the Central Committee which was to convene the next day to discuss industrial modernization and automation. "Some Soviet engineers," he said, "are producing machines that are just no good." He said he was going to bring pressure on the engineers and designers to build better machinery for Soviet farms and factories. "I am going to collect some of the worst examples and exhibit them in a sort of Hall of Shame." Beside the bad examples he would put good machines. This, he thought, would shame the designers into improving their work.

However, he added, he was having trouble laying his hands on the bad models. "Apparently the designers know what I have in mind, because they are not sending them into Moscow and I'm having to send special people to collect them." I expressed surprise, saying I thought his word was law in the Soviet Union. "It is," he said blandly, "but there's always a way of getting around the law."

Again I was struck with the contrast to Stalin. When the latter's inspectors found badly designed machines they called it sabotage, and the punishment for that was all too often liquidation.

As I thought back to Stalin and watched the affable, self-assured man lolling relaxed beside me, talking volubly about his plans to persuade his countrymen to make greater efforts to achieve Communism's goals, I wondered whether his new techniques were going to succeed.

Khrushchev has, of course, one great advantage which Stalin was only beginning to enjoy when he died—the threat of economic penalty. A destitute man has no fear of being deprived of his possessions. When there is little to buy but bread, one's wages lose their significance. But today Soviet families are beginning to accumulate treasured possessions—clothing, furniture, even occasionally a bungalow. With their small salaries added together, a man and his wife can eke out a passable existence for themselves and their children.

Today to be deprived of one's salary can mean a drastic reduction in the way the entire family lives and eats. Where the state is the sole employer, this is a formidable weapon. The compulsion to conform to the regime's rules, written or unwritten, in order to preserve even the meager living standard of the average worker is considerable. But for the higher-salaried engineers, plant managers, writers and scientists the compulsion becomes all but irresistible.

As long as Soviet society is in this stage of precarious living, I believe that the desire for an apartment or a pair of shoes will outweigh any longing for the less tangible benefits of greater freedom. The average man will not jeopardize his chances of getting the former by brash demands for the latter.

However, I am inclined to believe that as the most immediate needs for material goods are met, there will be a growing demand for increasing liberty. As the demand spreads among groups whose services are indispensable to the economy, it will become a kind of collective bargaining which the regime cannot ignore indefinitely.

While there are no legal or constitutional restraints against the resumption of terror should the demands for greater freedom become excessive in the eyes of the Communist leaders, I believe that a restoration of the Stalinist system of rule by fear would produce repercussions which the boldest and most ruthless Kremlin leader would shrink from facing.

It is for these reasons that I found in Khrushchev's lessening of terror as a means of ruling, the most encouraging change since the days of Marshal Stalin.

CHAPTER NINE

Discipline

DURING THE WAR, to spur arms production, Stalin had imposed harsh labor laws enforcing discipline in the factories. These laws were still in effect when I left the Soviet Union in 1946. For being twenty minutes late at work, people were hauled before the criminal courts and fined up to twenty per cent of their wages for six months. For being absent from work or quitting their jobs they were liable to prison sentences or forced labor.

Since then these laws had lapsed and with Stalin's death they were rescinded. What had been the effect on labor discipline of these relaxations? This too was a field I was interested in when I returned to the Soviet Union. What I found was a little startling but effective.

When Stalin's labor laws were rescinded, I was told, it was for a time difficult to enforce labor rules within plants. Absenteeism and lax discipline increased. Instead of using the courts of law to remedy the situation, Soviet leaders sought other ways to induce workers to get to their jobs on time and to behave themselves.

In Leningrad Khrushchev's energetic appointee Mayor

Smirnov explained one of these ways to me. An old Communist institution of "Comradely Courts," he said, had existed in the twenties to deal with minor infractions of Communist social order but had apparently been too soft for Stalin's tastes and were replaced by more stringent law courts and the police. Smirnov had revived these Comradely Courts in Leningrad and since then the system had spread to other cities all over the country.

Essentially a Comradely Court is a public meeting of one's neighbors or fellow workers, convened without rules of evidence, defense attorneys or formal procedures, to deal with minor infractions of the rules of Communist society and labor. In each factory the Communist Party designates and the workers thereupon elect a "president," who with the assistance of two deputies "tries" cases before a miscreant's fellow workers.

Mayor Smirnov invited me to attend such a trial at the Leningrad steel mills. A hundred workers, men and women, from one of the shops were assembled in a room after their shift was over. At one end of the room, behind a large table, the president sat flanked by a woman and a man, one a machine operator, the other a fitter. Directly in front of him sat the defendant, dressed in a suit several sizes too large for him, so that his hands disappeared in the cuffs.

The proceedings opened with the president's reading the charge, which had been prepared in the office of the manager—that the defendant had skipped a shift, claiming he was sick. The defendant, following Soviet trial-court tradition, confessed fully but explained that after five days on the night shift he had caught the grippe. Since the factory clinic where sick leaves are granted was closed, he first tried to be transferred to an early shift so that he could get off by midnight and get a good night's sleep to throw off the grippe, but the shift boss had refused. Angry, the defendant went home to bed. Next day he found a doctor who certified that he had a high temperature and gave him some medicine. The following day he returned to work. The worker recognized that this was not a valid excuse for his transgression but he asked humbly that it be considered a mitigating circumstance.

The judge then asked the defendant's fellow workers what they thought. In turn several rose and denounced the offense as reflecting on the honor of the whole factory, but each recommended mercy. The miscreant, they testified, was a hard worker and had even recently been given a prize for overfulfilling his norm. Only one fellow worker had a criticism—the man did not fulfill his social duties, i.e., he did not attend party lectures and gatherings.

When the fellow workers had finished, the judge asked, "What punishment shall we give him?" Someone suggested he be reprimanded and another seconded the motion. The judge and his assistants withdrew for a few minutes and then returned to read the verdict: reprimand. The defendant arose, thanked the Comradely Court for its leniency and promised that he would prove he had learned his lesson by working even better in the future.

After the "trial" one of Leningrad's leading jurists explained to me the functions and duties of the Comradely Courts. They are, he said, completely outside the regular court system. They have strictly limited jurisdiction and powers of punishment. Besides issuing reprimands they can recommend to management that a delinquent be demoted to a poorer-paying job or in extreme cases fired. In the case of infractions of social order in an apartment house or dwelling, they can recommend that the police refuse him a residence permit and thus effectively banish the guilty man from the city. Amendments were being considered authorizing Comradely Courts to impose fines up to 100 rubles.

I asked the jurist whether these extralegal measures were not causing concern among legal experts, as I had heard elsewhere that they are. He said that, on the contrary, judges found them a godsend, as they relieved the court calendar of many trivial cases, including petty theft. Calling to mind the people's courts of the French Revolution, I pointed out the defendant obviously had the sympathy of his fellow workers, but what happened if an unpopular worker were tried by an unsympathetic crowd? The jurist stated that every sentence was subject to appeal to the local town council, which could annul unjust punishments.

The director of the plant stated that the institution of Comradely Courts had been one of the most effective ways of maintaining labor discipline. A delinquent, he argued, would often rather appear before a regular judge in a closed court and be sentenced to several days in jail than be held up to scorn and shame by his fellows in a Comradely Court.

I came away from the experience with mixed opinions. Clearly these trials by mob had little in common with Anglo-Saxon principles of justice. Clearly too, they were used almost entirely by management as a device for enforcing stringent discipline. Where was the line between forced labor and a system in which skipping a single shift was considered an offense? The humble confession and the promise to do better by the delinquent worker reminded me more of a child being called before a boys'-school student council than the reaction of a grownup man.

Mayor Smirnov of Leningrad also introduced me to still another innovation in the maintenance of law and order. "Hooliganism," he told me, has long been a curse of peaceful citizens in Leningrad. Gangs of rowdies haunted parks, movie houses, sports stadiums and other places where crowds congregated on holidays and not only abused the holidaymakers but often picked their pockets and even manhandled them. Six or eight months before my visit a young Moscow University student on vacation in Leningrad had tried to remonstrate with a gang of hooligans and had been stabbed to death. The hooligans were caught and shot, but the case had aroused such public indignation that Smirnov had authorized the formation of a sort of auxiliary police.

Recruited under the supervision of the Komsomol organization, these volunteers are given badges and identity cards authorizing them to maintain order in public places, to take the identity of offenders against the peace and even to deliver recalcitrants to the police station. (Mayor Smirnov insisted that this differed from the right to arrest, though I failed to find any great distinction.) The volunteers, who work three or four hours each month without pay, are assigned to patrol public places in squads varying in size from four or five on quiet days to as many as fifteen or twenty on Saturdays and Sundays.

At the Leningrad electric-generator plant I met four of the three hundred active auxiliaries in the plant, who told me enthusiastically about their activities. Their leader was a full-time Communist Party worker, but several were not even members of the party. One of them, a young engineer who spoke excellent English, explained why he had volunteered: "I was tired of having my girl friend insulted and abused by foul language every time we went out for a walk in the park."

He also said that an auxiliary is expected to maintain order even when he is not on duty. "The other day I took my girl to a very nice ice-cream parlor on Nevski Prospekt," he said, and he added parenthetically that I should go there myself while I was in Leningrad. "A drunk came in and began throwing his weight around and insulting the customers. So I took him by the scruff of the neck and threw him out. If I hadn't been so busy, I would have taken him to the police station."

When Mayor Smirnov told me of his force of seventeen thousand auxilaries, which he hopes to expand to fifty thousand, I asked whether private citizens did not resent this unofficial police force. Were the auxiliaries not in effect vigilantes who might exceed their authority and interfere in others' private affairs? But the mayor dismissed the objection flatly. They were carefully screened, he said, and were well briefed before they went on patrol. While excesses were always possible in any such organization, they were unlikely. "After all, every Leningrader has been to high school." He added that the auxiliaries had been so successful that he had been able to cut his police force by thirty per cent. Other cities too had adopted the system and only recently he had received a report from Sverdlovsk in the Urals saying it had done wonders to reduce public disorder. He was evidently very proud of the organization and before I left he presented me with an identity card as an honorary auxiliary and pinned the auxiliary badge on my coat.

Like the Comradely Courts, the auxiliary police force raised questions in my mind. I had already read in the Soviet newspapers veiled complaints from legal authorities criticizing this somewhat casual method of maintaining order. However, this question seems to be related to that of drunkenness, which is a special problem in the U.S.S.R. As in all northern countries, alcoholic consumption is heavy and for generations drunkenness has been common. In the Soviet Union a drunk is generally considered a public ward rather than a pest. If one falls into a snowdrift on a cold night it is the sacred duty of the public to get him home. Only when the drunk misbehaves is he transgressing the proprieties. I gathered that such drunks are the special objective of the auxiliaries.

"We consider our chief task educational, not punitive," one of them told me. "Only a very small fraction of those we handle are taken to the police station. Our job is to set an example and to persuade."

The Comradely Courts and the police auxiliaries are, I believe, characteristic of Khrushchev's determined effort to substitute persuasion for compulsion. To Anglo-Saxons these methods might, as I suggest, cause apprehension. But in a country where legality plays a far more modest role in government, only a small circle of legal experts seems to be disturbed. Thus far, Khrushchev's new methods appear to be popular at least among the plant managers and are obviously much less oppressive than Stalin's fearful labor laws.

CHAPTER TEN

Ferment

THE LESSENING of terror after Stalin's death seemed to provoke a chain reaction. In Poland, Hungary and Germany, students and writers had revolted. In Moscow, too, writers and students had shown signs of restlessness interpreted by some abroad as the first indications that a political upheaval among Soviet intellectuals was imminent.

These were among the reports I was eager to look into when I went back to Moscow. Although I found such reports exaggerated, there is considerable ferment among intellectuals which I feel is encouraging.

From the beginning of the Revolution, it had been a basic principle of Lenin that intellectual activities in the Soviet Union were to be tolerated only to the extent that they served the immediate purposes of the regime. Indeed, even before the Revolution the Communists had unashamedly made use of liberal writers and thinkers to further their interests, only to jettison them like useless ballast when the Revolution was over.

Stalin had sharpened the dictum of "usefulness" to its

harshest extreme. The Soviet intelligentsia, he directed, was to write books or plays, paint pictures and compose music according to a prescribed formula which conformed strictly to his views of what was useful and aesthetic. The model for all was called "socialist realism," which meant depicting Soviet life as a photographic reproduction of what Communism was supposed to be like.

The fables, morality plays and Communist religious pictures which resulted were not only sterile but excessively boring. Anti-Soviet villains and Communist heroes repeated their defeats and victories with deadly monotony, while fictional farm girls fell in love with their tractors and their fictional brothers in the factories tripled their work norms.

When Stalin died and the first amnesties and signs of relaxation appeared, some writers and poets thought the great thaw in the frozen intellectual life of the country was under way. One well-known writer, Ilya Ehrenburg, who had been a faithful adherent of socialist realism, even wrote a short novel entitled *The Thaw.* But the Kremlin leaders soon disabused them and word went out that socialist realism was still the law.

The great majority of writers conformed, but a handful were brash enough to defy the edict. A young and unknown writer, Dudintsev, wrote *Not by Bread Alone,* a mediocre novel which, however, created a sensation among Soviet readers because for the first time it depicted the Soviet bureaucracy as an obstacle to individual achievements. Though Dudintsev was severely criticized and for a time fell into disfavor, a number of other writers managed to get similarly advanced ideas published in Soviet literary journals.

Forewarned by the Polish writers' revolt and the Hungarian revolution which followed, Khrushchev called his intellectuals to order again. Some recanted but others maintained a sullen silence. Khrushchev summoned them to his country house and read them a lecture in such vivid language that one of the writers, a woman, is reported to have fainted. Reduced in numbers, the recalcitrant writers nevertheless continued their "campaign of silence," and even today a number of them are still stubbornly holding out.

Meantime, Boris Pasternak wrote his famous novel *Dr. Zhivago,* which, we all know, was turned down for Soviet publication as a violation of the rules of socialist realism. When a smuggled copy was published abroad, he was roundly denounced but, in accordance with the new post-Stalin rules, not physically persecuted. He is still living comfortably in his *dacha* in the country.

During my visit to Moscow another congress of writers was held and was addressed by Khrushchev himself. His speech was a masterpiece of persuasion. He told the writers he could not tell them how to write novels. He flattered them and cajoled but did not order them what to write. Most significant of all, the words "socialist realism" were scarcely mentioned.

Does this mean that Khrushchev has given in? Does it mean that from now on Soviet writers will be free to ignore the Communist Party's instructions about what to write? At present, certainly not.

As in other fields, Khrushchev is loosening the reins on the intellectuals. Doubtless the definition of socialist realism will be broadened. Those who violate the rules will not be persecuted and sent to Siberia, as hundreds were under Stalin. But they remain subject to other reprisals.

Ever since the Revolution, writers and artists have been among the highest-paid of all professionals. They have enjoyed many special privileges like country houses and even private cars, and they have been permitted to travel abroad. But their chief rewards have been the high royalties they collect when their books are published in hundreds of thousands of copies. It takes but a slight raising of an eyebrow to persuade a government publisher not to publish a book, thus depriving a writer of the large income he has become accustomed to receiving. Perhaps some can get along on their savings, but in the end the great majority will surrender and once more write, or paint or compose, what the Communist Party thinks best.

However, the unrest which has appeared among the writers is not confined to this small group. Academicians, professors and teachers, I found, are also beginning to express doubts about some of the alleged scienctific dogmas of Marxism. This ferment, I believe, is even more active among Soviet youth.

In the universities and higher technical schools there is wide indifference to Communist ideology. The interminable classes in dialectical materialism and Marxism-Leninism which students are required to take year after year have evoked undisguised boredom and impatience among the younger generation. Nor is their attitude always a passive one. In classrooms, at student conferences, and in Communist Party gatherings, they are openly asking questions about the accuracy of "scientific Marxism" and about some of Marx's basic conclusions, questions which their instructors find it embarrassing to answer satisfactorily.

As a result, some students, I am told, are beginning to entertain serious doubts about the intellectual qualifications of their leaders who are endlessly parroting and blindly following doctrines which they believe are demonstrably in conflict with facts. Even in matters of foreign affairs, Marxist dogma on the inevitable decay of capitalism is becoming more difficult to reconcile with conditions abroad. As Soviet students learn more and more about life beyond the Communist frontier their skepticism is inevitably increasing. Though their natural patriotism and their pride in the material achievement of their country lead them to reject any unfavorable comparisons between the Soviet Union and other countries, they are finding it hard to accept the intellectual authority and infallible judgment of their own leaders, to a degree that is clearly worrying Mr. Khrushchev himself.

Stalin was educated as a theologian in a Tiflis seminary. Though he was contemptuous of intellectuals as he was of most professions—he was educated enough not to be envious of them. Khrushchev told me that he himself started working as a shepherd at the age of seven. Perhaps he was able to finish a few years of school before he went to work in the mines, where he stayed until the Revolution. It is doubtful therefore that he had any systematic education except what he got at the special Communist Party leadership schools after the Revolution—and this could hardly be called a well-rounded liberal education.

Under these circumstances it would be extraordinary if Khrushchev did not have a certain resentment for and suspicion of intellectuals—of anyone who finished college. Like every good Communist he believes strongly in education, including college education, and he has encouraged the building of schools almost as much as that of living quarters during his regime, but he regards education as a utilitarian contribution to the aims of the Communist state rather than as a personal contribution to the student's development. To educate more people than the state can use or to give a student more knowledge than can be usefully exploited is, to him, not just a waste of energy but a potential source of trouble—like the overproduction of wheat in the United States.

An American once asked Stalin whether he was not educating himself out of a job—whether an enlightened public might reject his system. Stalin curtly dismissed the question.

"We are a dark people," was a favorite expression of the Russian masses prior to the Revolution. Elementary schooling, while expanding, was available to only five to twenty-five per cent of the children, varying in different parts of Russia. But today illiteracy has been all but abolished. Every child is required to finish a seven-year primary and secondary schooling. A ten-year school has up to now been obligatory in urban areas.

College education has been expanded dramatically, for Stalin and Khrushchev were well aware that without trained scientists, engineers and economists they would never achieve their industrial goals. But the increase in universities and polytechnic institutes has not kept pace with the growing number of high-school graduates. Soviet Minister of Higher Education Elutin told me that there are three applicants for every vacancy in college, including night and correspondence. Though there are one and a half million high-school graduates each year, there are only 260,000 vacancies for full-time college students. However, Minister Elutin said the number of annual vacancies is being expanded to 300,000. He also told me that an equal number of students would take correspondence and night courses.

There are several reasons for this discrepancy in the otherwise totally planned economy of the Soviet Union. The rector of the University of Moscow admitted to me that there was a serious shortage of teachers for college courses. He also pointed out that the mere physical problem of expanding university capacity was immense. But a more important reason for the discrepancy is that the Soviet leaders have calculated that they do not need more college graduates in the coming years. Hence the capacity of the universities is being deliberately kept down.

However, every parent and every student in Russia knows very well that education is the single most important criterion of future success in the Soviet Union. A seven-year-school graduate can climb the economic ladder only to a certain well-defined rung. A ten-year graduate can go a little higher. Those who go to vocational colleges can rise a few more steps but no further. The son of a general or of a well-paid factory official may land a soft job through pull, but his chances of advancement are small unless he has the certificates and diplomas which the upper rungs of success require.

The pressure to get into college is therefore enormous, and parents as well as students go to any lengths to wangle admissions. While I was in the Soviet Union, a number of college officials in Kiev were under investigation for accepting bribes from parents to arrange for their children's admission to the local university. The bribes ran to several thousand rubles. Later I read that the erring officials had been heavily fined but oddly enough the students whose admissions they had arranged were not punished. The case was not at all unusual and I am told similar cases are constantly being aired in the Soviet press.

Wealthy parents can also smooth the way to college for their offspring by bribing the examiners who mark the entrance examinations. However, this method is going to be more difficult in the future. Minister Elutin has told me that beginning next year all entrance examination papers will be numbered and not signed so that the examiner will not know whose paper he is marking.

A third way for parents to help their children is to hire special tutors to cram students before entrance exams. I asked a schoolmistress in Kiev if this was common. She was a good Communist but she reluctantly admitted that "some do." From other quarters I heard it was a generally accepted practice.

I was told by one source that a quarter of the students in Soviet universities today owe their admissions to pull. This figure may be exaggerated. But the energetic efforts of Mr. Khrushchev to combat the practice, especially in the recent school reforms, indicate that parents' wealth and position are being used to a great extent to help their children get into college and thus into well-paying, respected jobs so that they will not have to become laborers.

Mr. Khrushchev's concern is doubtless partly due to his fear that education will somehow become a monopoly of the upper strata of Soviet society. He probably also objects to graft and pull per se. But I think his main concern is to avoid the creation of an intellectual elite such as has always prevailed in more advanced European countries. The uprisings in Poland and the revolution in Hungary are due, he no doubt believes, to the existence of a student class, isolated from the working masses, who prided themselves on their independence of thought and their intellectual superiority over the political leaders who ruled them. He is determined that no such student class will arise in the Soviet Union to question his authority or evoke derisive comparisons between his meager education and theirs.

Some months before my trip Mr. Khrushchev made an important speech advocating that all high-school graduates should be required to spend two years working in factories before being admitted to college. He said that too many youngsters were afraid to get their hands dirty and had no respect for physical labor. What was more, they were supported by their parents, who wanted their children to pass from school to an office job without ever doing a stroke of demeaning physical labor. While Americans are worrying about overemphasis on life-adjustment courses in American schools, Mr. Khrushchev seems genuinely concerned that Soviet students are not being sufficiently adjusted to the main purpose of Soviet life—hard work.

The response to Mr. Khrushchev's proposals was as close to a mass protest as anything that has happened in the Soviet Union since the Revolution. Several highly placed members of the Academy of Sciences pointed out that in their fields of mathematics and physics it was essential that the educational process proceed uninterrupted from high school through university. Parents also expressed concern, but in more veiled forms.

In the end a compromise was reached and a new school reform was decreed. During my visit I made a special effort to study both the purposes and the effect of the reform. It soon became clear, however, that there were almost as many interpretations of the new law as there were professional educators.

In general, it was agreed that a large percentage—perhaps eighty per cent—of all high-school graduates would be required to do some form of practical work either before entering college or during their college careers. The average student would be required to go to a factory for two years after high school. During that period he might take college preparatory courses either from correspondence school or at night school. Otherwise he might only work and at the end of two years take refresher courses and then examinations for the university.

Some students, I was told at the university in Tashkent,

would be admitted directly from high school but during their college careers would be given "practical work," varying from six months to two years, in the university itself—as laboratory assistants, librarians or other odd jobs.

Finally, students in some subjects—notably mathematics and physics—would be permitted to skip the work period entirely. The rector of the University of Moscow, Professor Petrovski, explained to me that these students were badly needed by the state and that an interruption in their studies would set them back.

Minister Elutin said that students of the humanities— future lawyers, journalists, economists and philosophers— would greatly profit from experience in factories or on farms. "How can a judge properly discharge his duties un- less he has rubbed shoulders with other workers and labored with them in the workshop?" he said. Furthermore, both Elutin and Petrovski pointed out that two years of work between school and college tend to mature students and make them more eager to study. The same ex- perience was noted in America with many of our G.I. Bill students.

Another, less frequently cited reason for the reform is that it will relieve the pressure on the universities from the ever increasing number of high-school graduates. "Once they get into a factory many of them will get used to a worker's life, get married and settle down and forget their desire to go to the university," one high-school teacher told me.

Along with the reform in higher education, there is a major reform in the school system. Mr. Khrushchev's reform radically alters the secondary-school system. In place of the seven- and ten-year curricula there will be eight- and eleven-year curricula. The eight-year curriculum will be compulsory for all students. Those who hope to go to college or to a technical institute will go on for three additional years, possibly at regular day schools, with one third of the time spent in productive labor; but a large number, I gathered, will complete their college preparatory studies at night schools and correspondence schools while they work in a factory or on a farm.

In Kiev my wife and I visited a regular ten-year school and were shown through it by its vigorous little gray-haired headmistress, Nina Burichenko. Although she was educated under the Czars she is a staunch Communist and her bosom was resplendent with Soviet decorations. She runs her school, however, in what she herself described as a "guards officer manner." Mrs. Burichenko said she was already preparing the new curriculum provided for by the school reform. One measure was to consolidate a number of courses into one. For example, the history, geography and natural history of a country under study were to be taught from a single textbook. I gathered that the consolidation was due to the compressing of as much of the curriculum as possible into eight years. Mrs. Burichenko also stated that at present about twenty per cent of her pupils leave school after seven years, primarily for financial reasons—that is, the parents need the additional income.

Mrs. Burichenko also pointed out that because of the very stiff competitive examinations for college entrance, many students do not even try to go on to college. From last year's graduating class of fifty-six, twenty-four applied for admission to college and only nine made it—that is, one in seven. Although the Soviet Constitution guarantees the right to education for all, this did not disturb Mrs. Burichenko. It was far better, she said, for most of her students to go to work when they left her establishment, and start contributing to the building of Communist society.

Just how the Khrushchev school reforms are to be put into practice is still very vague. Every schoolteacher, university rector and ministerial official I discussed it with had different ideas about how it would work out—some of them almost diametrically opposed. When I pointed this out to a prominent educator he smiled indulgently and said he was not surprised. I asked him whether he thought it would achieve its aims. "Come back in three years and I'll tell you," he replied.

In addition to the school reform, Mr. Khrushchev has made another basic change in the school system—the introduction of boarding schools. Though he proposed this innovation only three years ago, there are already 180,000 boarding-school students in the Soviet Union. The announced purpose of these schools is to take care of the orphans and the children of invalids and poor families. Since probably the vast majority of women under sixty in the Soviet Union have jobs and live in inadequate quarters, the opportunity to send children away to boarding school is eagerly sought, and I would not be surprised if here too the same sort of pull and graft used to get children into college is not resorted to by influential parents of school-age children.

The boarding schools are also highly prized by Communist officials for quite another reason. Mayor Dynkin of Stalingrad said to me, "They not only provide the best way of educating children but they are the ideal method of raising the youth in the spirit of Communism with both collective study and collective living."

While I was traveling around the Soviet Union, the government announced plans for increasing the number of boarding schools. This new plan prescribes that by 1965 the number of schools will be increased fourteenfold to take care of two and a half million pupils.

The boarding schools take children from the first grade, at seven years. The Soviet authorities believe that children are too young before seven to go to school. At present they teach children through the tenth grade and when the new school reform comes they will presumably take them through the eleventh. The average school has six hundred students, who are generally housed in two dormitories of three hundred each. Parents may visit them or take them home on weekends and during holidays.

The University of Moscow is the Mecca of students from the entire Soviet bloc. Recently built on the old Sparrow Hills, later named Lenin Hills, where I had often skied when I was ambassador during the war, it rises white and shining above the city, replete with Grecian urns, heroic statues and slender spires topped with hammers and sickles. Here sixteen thousand students from all over the Soviet Union, China, Southern Asia and even the United States are studying under a staff of two thousand teachers, five hundred of them full professors.

I called on its rector, Professor Petrovski, in his sky-scraper office. Professor Petrovski told me that more than half his students study in the natural sciences and the rest in liberal arts. The university does not have an engineering or a medical faculty; these specialties are taught at separate institutes in Moscow. He said that physics and chemistry are the most popular of the sciences, and philology and journalism the most sought after among the liberal arts. He explained these latter preferences by pointing out that newspaper work and language studies were most likely to lead to foreign assignments.

In addition to his sixteen thousand full-time students,

Petrovski's staff teaches seven thousand more students in correspondence and night school courses. The widespread use of these methods of teaching, he explained, is due to the enormous thirst for education which Soviet workers all evince—a thirst which I found wherever I traveled in the Soviet Union. The correspondence students, I was told, are given an extra month off in addition to their regular leave from the enterprise in which they work, for laboratory experience, special lectures and examinations. In other universities, I was told, the time off was even greater, ranging all the way to three months at the University of Samarkand.

Diplomas for night school and correspondence graduates, Petrovski told me, are identical with the full-time student's diplomas. However, though full-time students have in the past completed their college education in five years, correspondence students have had to take six years.

In private conversations with students at Soviet universities I gained the impression that while the natural sciences are well taught and students in these disciplines are exceedingly devoted and hard-working, the humanities are less favored with gifted teachers, the courses are dull and replete with repetitive courses in Marxism-Leninism, and the students generally are less able and less keen than the natural-science students.

In addition to its thirty-nine universities, the Soviet Union maintains over seven hundred institutes for teaching and research. Some are attached to the Ministry of Higher Education in Moscow, others are attached to the ministries more directly concerned. Medical institutes, for example, are under the Ministry of Health.

Beyond the universities and technical institutes lie the highest goals to which a Soviet intellectual can aspire—the Academy of Sciences in Moscow and its associated academies in the fifteen republics and the other regional areas of the Soviet Union. Even in Stalin's day an academician was among the highest-paid and most respected members of society. Today he earns a salary higher than any other official, has a car of his own, a house in the country and a prestige second only to the top Kremlin leaders. When Khrushchev first suggested his radical reform of education it was two members of the U.S.S.R. Academy of Sciences who publicly warned him against going too far.

Wherever I could I visited the academies of the republics and invariably I found their members frank and by far the most independent of all the officials I met. They had risen, it seemed to me, as high above politics as anyone can in the Soviet Union and occasionally expressed frank skepticism about the wisdom of measures supported by even Khrushchev himself. Furthermore, their activities are not confined to abstruse academic problems but are intimately related to major problems of the country.

In an earlier chapter I recalled my visit to the Tadzhik Academy of Sciences. The practical role its members play in the development of the republic is illustrated by the vital problems its thirteen institutes are dealing with. Cotton is Tadzhikistan's principal source of revenue, and one institute of the academy is working almost exclusively on improving the strains of cotton which after proper testing are distributed among the state and collective farms. The fact that Tadzhikistan's average yield last year was 2,300 pounds of cotton per acre, which, it is claimed, is better than most comparable yields in California, indicates the progress they are making in this field.

Another problem is the improvement of grazing lands in the Pamir Mountains, which occupy about ninety per cent of Tadzhikistan's territory. At present they are developing new grasses and sowing the seed in the mountain pastures by airplane. A special problem has been to develop better forage for the yaks which are the chief form of transportation and an important source of milk and meat for the mountaineers in the remote valleys of eastern Tadzhikistan.

Among the important sources of revenue are the sheep herds which graze in the winter on the semiarid steppe and in summer are driven into the mountains. An institute of animal husbandry has done considerable research in improving local breeds and has developed the Gyar type, which reaches a weight of over four hundred pounds per head—the largest breed of sheep in the world, they claim.

An institute of seismology is not only studying the seismography of Tadzhikistan, where severe earthquakes are frequent, but is also working with engineers to develop building methods to resist these violent shocks.

Other scientists are grappling with the erosion problem in the mountain valleys, which they described to me as serious. An important weapon against erosion is afforestation. Since the Tadzhiks find it simpler to import building lumber from Siberia, they are developing fruit-bearing trees which can be sown in large quantities on the mountain slopes. What success they are having was not revealed.

In all, seven hundred Tadzhik scientists are working on these practical problems to improve their country's economy and exploit its considerable mineral resources.

When the academy itself was founded in 1951, there was scarcely a scientist of sufficient caliber to meet the high standards demanded of "academicians" in the Soviet Union. However, since then enough have risen to the top to occupy seventy per cent of the chairs, and the number is steadily increasing.

Academy President S. U. Umarov's own story is typical of many of his colleagues' rise to eminence in the scientific world. Left an orphan at an early age in the village of Kojent now Leninabad in northern Tadzhikistan, he finished fourth grade there and then managed to be sent by party officials to Tashkent to finish his schooling. There he won a scholarship to Leningrad University, where he studied for his doctorate. He is a theoretical physicist and in addition to heading the academy teaches at the university in Stalinabad but only for two hours a week. If he had a heavier schedule, he told me, it would detract from his research and experimental work.

In Tashkent I visited the Uzbek Academy of Sciences and talked to its president, Professor Abdulaev, a geologist. During the course of our conversation I asked him whether he had found American geological methods useful. Frankly, but almost apologetically, he told me that till the middle 1930s American geologists were considered leaders in the field. Their findings were cited in all Soviet textbooks and their books were studied by all advanced students. However, he said, since then, while they have not fallen back, they have lost their position of pre-eminence.

The reason was, he said with genuine regret, that they failed to keep up with developments in the field of geology and geophysics in the rest of the world. He mentioned the works of several Soviet scientists who in the past few years made important contributions to geology which were scarcely noted, let alone translated, in the United States. New methods of exploring the subsoil, he said, had recently been developed which American geologists simply ignored. He cited as examples methods of prospecting with electromagnetic photography and by the use of water analysis. Even the Chinese, he said, had made important advances with Soviet help which the Americans knew nothing of. This at any rate was what he told me.

He stated that he had discussed the question with American geologists at international conferences and had recommended to them the adoption of the Soviet system of collecting and abstracting every scientific paper published anywhere in the world. These abstracts are translated and distributed to all Soviet scientists with interests in that particular field. If they desire, the scientists can then get the original full text from the central collecting point in Moscow. "However," the little Uzbek scientist said sadly, "the Americans didn't follow our advice."

At another branch academy of sciences I raised the question of the virgin lands—the steppes being plowed up at the suggestion of Mr. Khrushchev—and I expressed agreement with Mr. Khrushchev that dust bowls seemed unlikely. A learned member of the academy across the table smiled. "It hasn't happened yet," he said cautiously. I pressed him further: "Do you think it might happen?" He shrugged his shoulders skeptically and said, "The problem requires further study." It was the first time in thirty years I had heard a responsible Soviet citizen cast doubt on the judgment of the supreme leader in front of a number of people, including a foreigner.

In the mountains behind Alma-Ata, close to the Chinese frontier, I visited one evening the High-Altitude Astronomical Research Institute of Professor Fesenkov, a member of the Soviet Academy of Sciences and an astronomer of world-wide reputation. With him were a number of postgraduate students of astronomy. Speaking English without the aid of an interpreter, Professor Fesenkov explained as best he could to a layman the intricate work he was doing in the field of astrophysics. He told about his expedition through the wilds of eastern Siberia in the dead of winter to investigate a shower of meteorites which had fallen in February 1947, devastating a forest area of several square miles. He showed me films of how, with the most primitive equipment, he had unearthed huge meteorites of iron, nickel and cobalt, some of them weighing several tons.

Fesenkov also told of his work in connection with the International Geophysical Year and the tracking of Soviet satellites. He told me he was working on an intricate theory of atmospheric optics, about which I am frank to confess I understood little. Afterward, as the light faded, he took me around the observatories. Below us the lamps of Alma-Ata shone brightly. He looked down at them angrily and said, "They are interfering with my observations." For a moment I wondered whether in its quest for scientific supremacy the Soviet government would move the city of Alma-Ata to some spot where it would not bother its leading astronomer.

Later when I returned to Moscow I visited another famous institute—the Institute of World Economics and International Relations. This is the establishment which studies economic conditions around the globe and provides the statistical data on which Mr. Khrushchev and his colleagues can chart the future course of world history according to Karl Marx.

I asked Professor Arzumanyan, the head of the institute, how he reconciled the predictions of Karl Marx on the decay of capitalism with the realities of American economic life. He replied that the predictions were being fulfilled on schedule, and his thirty or forty fellow economists who had congregated in his office for the meeting all murmured warm approval. He then delivered a lecture on the slowing down of the American economy and on why he and his colleagues were projecting only a two per cent increase in our future growth, hardly greater than our population increase. He argued that eventually it would lead to stagnation and then decay, with rising unemployment.

When he had finished, another economist posed a number of questions opposing my assertion that there was vast room for economic expansion in the United States and that our economy was in its most dynamic period. Our more conservative economists were estimating at least a three per cent increase in our gross national product while others, who I believe were more accurate, were projecting a four and a half per cent increase. The subsequent discussion, in which other members of the institute participated, indicated such a lack of understanding of American economic realities that I finally suggested that the members of the institute should review their findings more carefully lest they, like other Soviet economists before them, lose their jobs for inaccurate predictions about the American economy.

Khrushchev used the same figures as these economists in asserting that our economy was slowing down. I told him that our democratic life was in its most creative stage, with a vast potential in social and economic gains. I warned him that his economists were dangerously wrong in miscalculating our future growth. Khrushchev took violent exception to this, and Mikoyan joined him. They maintained that by Marxist doctrine they could analyze the American future better than we could.

The Institute of World Economics is not the only so-called scientific research institute whose objectivity has been warped by political ideology. In the purely scientific field of genetics I also found Marxist dogma overriding sound scholarship. The teachings of the agronomist Lysenko on the inheritance of acquired characteristics have been rejected universally by reputable scientists everywhere—including many in the Soviet Union. Yet because these teachings are better suited to Marxism—and perhaps because Khrushchev thinks they yield quick short-term results—Lysenko has won the support of the Kremlin leaders, and several of his fellow scientists who opposed his views were removed from their posts on the editorial board of the official journal shortly after my return from Russia.

In the technical and scientific fields there can be no doubt that the Soviet educational system has thus far served its practical purposes admirably in the interest of the Soviet state; the sputniks and the nuclear bombs have testified to this. Whether the changes Mr. Khrushchev has introduced will improve or damage it remains to be seen—as at least one prominent Soviet educator indicated.

The academies of sciences scattered throughout the country have also, it seems to me, played an invaluable role in the development of the Soviet Union's material resources. However, I have grave reservations whether the system has done as much in the development of her most important resource—her people.

From what I could see, it seemed to me that in the field of natural sciences and in philology the system was training highly qualified specialists in many important areas, though without giving them a rounded education. However, in the humanities, especially history and economics, where Marxist dogma is at stake (as in the Institute of World Economics), I found on the contrary that truth was being sacrificed to doctrine. Nowhere did I find Soviet students offered the opportunity of obtaining a liberal education designed to develop well-rounded individuals.

Throughout the system—including the academies—I had the further impression that the emphasis on working in limited fields, whether in an observatory in the distant Altai Mountains on China's border or in a laboratory in Moscow, had produced an over specialization and a cleft between teaching and research which left little room for the unrestricted, individually creative scientific mind which, in the past, has usually produced the world's greatest discoveries.

Aside from the technical and organizational qualities of the Soviet educational and scientific-research system, I believe that the political problems Soviet educators are facing are of even more far-reaching importance. As education spreads and knowledge grows, the thirst for more knowledge inevitably increases. Since knowledge is probably the greatest enemy of false propaganda, the Communist Party's controllers of thought are finding their task more and more difficult.

It is still possible by constant reiteration to put across some falsehoods, such as, for example, the alleged aggressive nature of American policy. But with each class that graduates from Soviet high schools the demand for more information and the unwillingness to accept unsubstantiated dogmas increase. The process is a slow one, but I believe that in the long run it holds out for us more promise than almost any other development I found in the Soviet Union.

CHAPTER ELEVEN

Circuses

MR. KHRUSHCHEV had told me that America had made such profits out of two world wars that it had been able to bribe its workers to postpone a revolution.

Recalling the endless circuses, parks of culture and rest, palaces of culture and palaces of health I had visited in the past six weeks, I was tempted to reply that Mr. Khrushchev himself had not done a bad job of bribing his workers with circuses to take their minds off the conditions under which they are existing.

Travelers returning from the Soviet Union in recent years have said that, despite the improvement in living conditions, life was so dreary, drab and dismal that the people would not take it for long. Whether or not I wanted to look into the countermeasures the Soviet authorities are taking against this dreariness, they were thrust upon me for examination by every mayor wherever I stopped. Though many of these efforts to brighten Soviet life were almost pathetically threadbare, others I found were in some respects superior to our own.

No visitor to the Soviet Union can deny that, compared

to the United States, life is indeed very drab for the Soviet citizen. However, the Communist rulers have provided some compensations which cannot be overlooked. The most important of these have been to relieve the average working-man from some of the worries and burdens which might plague him in a free society.

Although medical care is neither as thorough nor as skilled as that available to those who can afford it in our country, it is free for everyone. Every village has its clinic, every town its hospitals. On a collective cotton farm near Tashkent where two generations ago there was not even a trained nurse, my wife and I visited a maternity home which was as spotless and well run as any we found in the entire Soviet Union. In Stalingrad there was a special school for incurably backward children and in the suburbs a special sanatorium for tubercular children. The general practitioners who run the clinics and hospitals are not as thoroughly trained as many of ours, but they are available where a few years ago there were none, and their services are invariably free. No matter how poor the family, it is relieved of the anxiety at least of the doctors' bills which a sudden illness, a pregnancy or an accident might involve.

As I have already noted, housing in the Soviet Union is short and shoddy. But, in compensation, rents are low and evictions rare. The average rent of a workingman is seldom over five per cent of his income. Crowded and unsanitary though their dwellings are, Soviet citizens seldom need worry where next month's rent is coming from.

Although the freedom of a worker to choose his job is limited, steady employment is another recompense the Russians enjoy. In the Soviet planned economy unemployment is virtually unknown except for special cases, such as that of high-school graduates who are reluctant to take a job in a factory and hang about waiting for an opening in a more respectable office or ministry. Although under Stalin pensions were very inadequate, Khrushchev has raised them considerably, so that old age has lost at least some of its misery. While I would hardly call the Soviet pension scale generous, I found one party worker who had been retired for sickness getting a pension of $120 a month—which is a substantial sum according to Soviet standards.

In addition to these meager but often helpful material compensations for the dull life the worker must lead, the Soviet Union has devoted considerable effort ever since the Revolution to brightening his leisure time with recreation and entertainment. The most widespread of these efforts are the "parks of culture and rest."

When I first heard about these parks of culture and rest during my visit to the Soviet Union in 1926, I thought at first my interpreter was joking. Actually both the idea and the name were suggested by the great Russian writer Maxim Gorki, who became a Communist in his later years. Perhaps we have expressions which translated sound as odd to Russian ears.

These parks, as everyone who has visited Russia knows, are in fact areas of green and woodland usually close to the center of town. Their entrance is usually marked by a wooden latticework triumphal arch with fading paint, plastered with slogans such as "Rest is the right of every Soviet Citizen (U.S.S.R. Constitution)."

Inside, gravel paths lead under shady trees or across lawns of unkept grass. In all my travels in the Soviet Union I never once saw a simple lawnmower, to say nothing of a power mower. Instead I found hordes of old women with primitive sickles or shears trimming the grass in the parks and gardens.

Standard equipment for a park of culture and rest includes volleyball courts, concrete dance floors, an outdoor stage for concerts and theatricals, rostrums from which representatives of the party's Agitation Section can address the crowds, a reading room, a quiet corner where chess-players can gather, and a children's village, usually with a children's railroad.

Since visitors to the parks are supposed to absorb political indoctrination while they rest, there is often a central square where giant photographs of leading Soviet figures are displayed. "The people should have an opportunity to know who their leaders are," the deputy mayor of Alma-Ata explained to me.

In Samarkand I was taken to the park one evening by the mayor and the local Intourist representative. A small admission fee was being asked but the mayor told me the city council had just passed a resolution, to take effect the following week, abolishing the fee. On one side of the main walk was a gallery of the present members of the Soviet Presidium, the Soviet Union's highest ruling group. Opposite was a gallery of famous Russian writers—Pushkin, Chekhov, Lermontov and the Communist poet Mayakovsky. The Intourist representative pointed to these portraits and said, "It has always struck me as odd that practically every great Russian writer met a tragic end. Pushkin was killed in a duel, Chekhov died of tuberculosis, a broken man. Mayakovsky shot himself." I looked across the way at the Presidium members and wondered whether it had ever occurred to my guide that the same might be said of most of their predecessors.

At the far end of the park a large crowd had collected to watch a family of Tadzhik tightrope walkers perform on a high wire stretched above them. The crowd stood in a circle and the small children sat in front of them. The act, I was told, is an ancient Tadzhik form of entertainment. While one member of the troupe performs feats high above the crowd's heads another member in a clown's costume carries on a running dialogue with him, accompanied by the crowd's roars of laughter. Most of the talk was in Tadzhik but occasionally a joke in Russian was thrown in. At the end of the act, the watchers toss coins into the ring or pass them to the little children in front, who toddle forward and drop them in the performers' hats.

In another section of the park a band of native musicians was playing Central Asian music on strange-looking tambourines and stringed instruments while the audience listened from benches under the lime trees. In another circle a couple of young men were demonstrating tricks and feats of strength. The mayor told me all the performers were paid by the city council.

In Yalta I saw another type of mass entertainment on a more elaborate scale—the rest homes and sanatoria where tens of thousands of workers go each year for vacations and rest cures. I revisited Livadia, where I had stayed with President Roosevelt during the Yalta Conference. Once the summer palace of the Czars, it now houses nine hundred convalescents and holidaymakers. The Czar's ballroom, which we had used as the conference hall, is now a dining room. The Czar's bedroom is now a dormitory where ten women were living. In the room I had occupied were four miners from the Donbas who greeted me warmly.

Under the supervision of a staff of doctors and nurses, these vacationers lead strictly regulated lives, their hours of rest and relaxation carefully scheduled, their diets precisely formulated. While a few found this routine dull, others, I am sure, got great satisfaction out of the luxurious life they imagine was once led only by the Czar.

Livadia is but one of hundreds of sanatoria stretching along the Black Sea coast for hundreds of miles from Odessa to the Caucasus Mountains. Not far from Yalta I visited the former Vorontsev Palace, where Prime Minister Churchill had lived during the conference. Part of it is a museum and part a rest home. Nearby I was taken to a giant new sanatorium, the Ukraina, where hundreds of convalescents recuperating from nervous and lung diseases were enjoying a rest cure. Its imitation-marble stars and stuccoed statuary rose from the seashore in grandiose imitation of former imperial splendor.

Each year, I was told, over four hundred thousand lucky workers from all over the country come to Yalta and even more to Sochi to enjoy the warm sun and semitropical climate of the Black Sea. The standard vacation lasts twenty-four days and costs about $160. Sometimes the trade-unions pay as much as seventy per cent of this amount for lucky recipients of a sanatorium holiday. Wealthier individuals can arrange their vacations independently and pay the sum themselves if they have the pull to get a reservation. In the country nearer the large cities there are many similar rest homes and sanatoria.

In addition to the sick and invalids, resorts like Yalta and Sochi cater to a new class of vacationers from the pioneer settlements of Siberia. Hundreds of engineers and skilled workers have been lured, by high salaries and fat premiums, to those remote areas to build dams and factories. They are kept on the job for two years at a stretch and then granted vacations for as much as six months. With their accumulated savings which they have been unable to spend in the pioneer camps, they come to the warm Soviet

Riviera to indulge themselves after their grim tours in the cold north for as long as their fat rolls of bills hold out—much as the prospectors and pioneer cattlemen from our West once congregated in Chicago to blow their earnings on a spree. They frequent the souvenir shops along the seaside promenade and the restaurants and cafés, where dance bands are permitted to play "good" American jazz and where they can pass their evenings over bottles of locally made champagne and even Pilsner beer.

Since the death of Stalin, a growing number of select members of the Soviet upper crust—top officials, writers, actors, ballerinas—have been permitted to take their vacations abroad, many of them in such resorts as Karlsbad in Communist Czechoslovakia, once a favorite watering place of Europe's aristocracy. A smaller number are even permitted beyond the Iron Curtain to Europe and America. The Soviet travel agency Intourist arranges group tours of Western cities for highly paid engineers and executives. As a precaution against possible desertion such vacationers are seldom allowed to take their immediate families with them. Though occasionally a member of these tours does defect, the great majority are apparently quite content to return to their own country—another evidence of the growing acquiescence of the Soviet population with their Communist regime.

Sports is a major field of Soviet amusement. Soccer is the chief spectator sport. The major teams are sponsored by factories or other organizations and divided into A and B leagues. The players are technically amateurs and have jobs in the sponsoring organization. However, some of the top players are popular heroes and their actual jobs are often only nominal. Periodic complaints in the Soviet press indicate that their amateur status is sometimes not even nominal. Thus, for example, a champion forward may be employed by a factory as a physical-education instructor and probably does little besides train and play.

One of the best Soviet teams is Dynamo, organized by the Moscow automobile plant ZIL. Its manager told me he was an ardent fan and never missed a game. Dynamo is currently at the top of the A League. In the provincial cities I visited, all the top officials are keenly aware of the standing of the local team and told me that local loyalties are so intense that when the team loses the mayor is apt to get the blame. In Tashkent the Prime Minister told me his team was in the B League but he promised that if I came back in two years it would have made the A League. I was also told that occasionally a town or a factory steals a good player from another organization, but this practice is officially very much frowned upon.

The best players are as much heroes among young Russians as a baseball player in America. Visiting a Pioneer camp of ten-year-olds deep in the Siberian forest, I asked one youngster how good his soccer team was. "It's great," he told me, bursting with pride. "The goalie could show Yashin a thing or two." Yashin is the top goalkeeper of the Soviet Union.

Participant sports are also very much encouraged. Every college student is required to take 136 hours of sports during his first two years. However, there are few college teams such as those in America, and competitive sports are organized by clubs rather than by schools. An exception is rowing, in which crews from the various universities compete against each other. In their turn the clubs are subordinated to the Sports Committee of the U.S.S.R. The committee, incidentally, also has jurisdiction over chess, which is similarly organized into clubs. When I asked why chess was under the Sports Committee I was told, "What would you put it under, the Ministry of Health?"

Even in such individual sports as skiing or hunting the collective principle is maintained, and skiing clubs and hunting societies organize group practice, competition and other activities.

In many cities I was taken to the local Palace of Pioneers. Often, as in Leningrad and Sverdlovsk, these are the former palaces of the Czarist aristocracy and their elaborate decorations have been carefully preserved. They offer the school children everything from group games and dancing to model-airplane building and chess. In the summer, many of these organizations maintain large children's camps in the country. Because of these facilities and activities practically every Soviet child becomes a member of the Pioneers.

The most impressive of all Soviet entertainment activities is in the cultural field. Every city of a few thousand inhabitants has its opera house and theater where professional theatrical groups can perform or amateur theatricals take place. In Tashkent, with a population of four hundred thousand, there are seven theaters and the newly built opera house puts on over two hundred performances of ballet or opera each year.

The Russians have always had a talent approaching genius for theater. The Moscow Art Theater has for decades been one of the greatest theaters in the world. Its performances of Chekhov and Gorki are unsurpassed anywhere. The Russians are also highly musical and enjoy opera enormously. When my wife asked the maid at the guest house where we were staying what present we could give her she spurned the long-playing jazz records and the nylon stockings we had brought from America and asked for a ticket to the local opera.

Ballet was originally imported from Italy by the Czars, but it is in Russia that the art has reached its peak. Every large town in the Soviet Union has its own ballet troupe. Many of the dancers are trained at the famous ballet schools of Moscow and Leningrad but today the provincial cities are starting their own schools. While the theater, the opera and the ballet in the provinces are not always of the same high standard as in Moscow or Leningrad they are excellent and are more widespread than in any other country in the world.

In Stalinabad we saw a performance of native ballet at the new and elaborate opera house, which seats three thousand. In front of me three mountaineers in their picturesque costumes sat on the edge of their chairs following every movement with the keenest delight. When the villain seemed to be getting the upper hand they stirred uneasily and booed vociferously but when the hero staged a comeback they clapped and cheered with enthusiasm. Unfortunately the ballet had a sad ending and the three left the opera shaking their heads dejectedly.

In Kiev we saw a performance of Ukrainian folk dancing by the Ukrainian State Dance Ensemble which was brilliantly produced and performed. Its director, Mr. Pavlo Virski, told me he had recently taken the troupe to Vienna, Paris and London, where they had had great success. He told me he had been invited to the United States but would have to postpone the visit, as he had already made arrangements for the troupe to tour through the Ukraine. He explained that his one hundred performers would spend more than five weeks traveling about the country, giving at least one outdoor performance each day before collective farmers; if it rained and the performance had to be held indoors they would have to give two performances to accommodate the crowds they expected. It was the first time the troupe was making such a tour, Mr. Virski told me, and he feared it was going to be a little strenuous for his dancers.

Thus, drab as life in the Soviet Union is compared to American standards, it is not entirely without its bright side. The high quality and ready accessibility of its theater, opera and ballet cannot be underestimated.

All these activities are heavily subsidized by the state. In Stalinabad I found seats to the opera ranging in cost from thirty cents to a dollar, but the mayor told me they cost the government an average of five dollars each. Actors and actresses, ballet dancers and opera singers are given high salaries. A leading ballerina in Stalinabad gets $300 a month (three times the wage of the average factory worker) for six performances. However, she usually performs two or three times more each month and for each extra performance she earns an additional $50.

The idea of individual effort or private amusement is contrary to the political doctrine of collectivism, and the dominant feature of all entertainment or amusement in the Soviet Union is collective activity. Whether you sing or fish, climb mountains or play chess, your fun will be organized for you by an officially sponsored club which in turn is part of a larger collective reaching right up to a central organization in Moscow directed by a section of the Communist Party.

The average worker seems to have acquiesced in having his fun organized for him by government agencies, but I do not believe he has yet been taught by the Communist Party propagandists to prefer it to individually devised pleasures in which his own initiative rather than government direction determines how he disposes of his leisure.

I asked one ardent young Communist whether he would like to spend his vacation at one of the highly organized luxurious sanatoria on the Black Sea. He shook his head vigorously. "My idea of a vacation is to go off to a village with my wife and just be alone for a while."

Bowing to this craving for individuality and privacy, the city fathers of Kiev and other towns have set aside areas in the suburbs where city dwellers can acquire little plots in which they can plant gardens and build tiny shacks. During my brief visit to the city it was made clear that this craving for privacy was not confined to a few individualistic recalcitrants from the Communist system. It was the top state planner of the Ukraine who excused himself early from a meeting with me by explaining that he had to go out and water the flowers in his private garden in the suburbs.

CHAPTER TWELVE

All-Out Competitive Coexistence

As WITH MANY other visitors to the Soviet Union, one of my first and strongest impressions was the craving for peace which obsesses every Soviet citizen. Together with it is the longing for friendly relations with the United States. Wherever I traveled I was greeted with the appeal "Peace and friendship." This was not simply a propaganda slogan. On the contrary, it seemed to spring spontaneously and sincerely from the crowds who gathered around me everywhere.

When I revisited Livadia Palace where the Yalta Conference had been held a group of Pioneers had been brought to welcome me and offer my wife and myself flowers and songs. When the Pioneers had gone, a group of convalescents in the palace came up to shake my hand and shouted, "Peace and friendship!" At a hydroelectric works in Stalingrad the young workers pressed around my car asking why we could not come to an agreement with Khrushchev. They too shouted, "Peace and friendship!" Far out in Siberia at the closing of the Angara River dam at Bratsk, the workers—mostly young people—nearly mobbed my party trying to shake hands with me. When I got into my car to drive off they picked up the rear wheels to prevent me from leaving.

On planes and trains, other passengers, recognizing me from wartime days, came up and almost invariably asked nostalgically why we could not re-establish the good relations that had prevailed during the time of our alliance in the war, when I had been ambassador. When we were flying from Leningrad to Kiev a general leaned across the aisle and said, "I remember you from your pictures during the war. When can we bring back those close relations we had then?" Every speech at the innumerable banquets offered me by local officials recalled my role in those days of co-operation against Hitler.

No American can help being impressed by the popular cry for peace. Many have found comfort in it and have drawn the conclusion that so long as the Soviet people want peace the danger of war is slight. Unfortunately I cannot share their reasoning. For alongside the desire for peace I found a much more disturbing conviction among the Soviet people. The massive Soviet propaganda machine has, I believe, convinced most Soviet citizens that the United States is the greatest threat to peace in the world today. Every issue of every newspaper, every speech by a Kremlin leader contains some reference to American warmongers who are prolonging the cold war, promoting the arms race and calling outright for preventive war.

Incredible though it may seem to Americans, we are regarded as the potential aggressors. Although public opinion, where it cannot be manipulated by the party's propagandists, can exercise a restraining influence on the Kremlin, it can play no role at all in the vital question of war or peace, I fear, so long as the Soviet propagandists enjoy a monopoly in dispensing world news. If the Communist leaders should find it to their convenience to warm the cold war, they will have the Soviet people behind them. There will be no question in the Soviet public's mind that the aggressor is the United States.

This disturbing fact makes it necessary, in weighing the future, to listen not to the cries of "Peace and friendship" of the Soviet people, but to the words and actions of their leaders. To permit ourselves to be deluded by the comforting craving of the population to avoid war might lead to fatal miscalculations on our part.

When I revisited Yalta, I recalled the agreements we had reached there with Stalin for peacetime co-operation. Although Yalta has since been greatly maligned, it was there that President Roosevelt and Prime Minister Churchill persuaded Stalin to subscribe to a joint policy for the liberated areas of Eastern Europe and to the establishment of freely elected governments in the areas overrun by the Soviet armies. When the American President and the British Prime Minister took Stalin at his word at the Crimean conference, they remembered that the year before at Teheran Stalin had agreed to launch a heavy offensive on the eastern front to coincide with the Anglo-American cross-Channel operations and thus pin down scores of German divisions which would otherwise have been diverted to oppose the western advance after the landings. And that time Stalin had kept his word.

At Yalta Stalin had also specifically agreed to "the earliest possible establishment through free elections of governments responsive to the will of the people" and to collaborate with the Western powers to "solve by democratic means the pressing political and economic problems" of Eastern Europe. If one remembers that at the time of the Yalta

Conference the Western armies were just recovering from the Battle of the Bulge while the Red Army was rapidly approaching Berlin, it is not surprising that the whole world, including Roosevelt and Churchill, was gratified by the results they achieved in the Crimea.

Historians will argue for many years why Stalin failed to carry out his commitments. But the fact remains that within weeks of the conference he began to go back on his promises. At Potsdam and at a series of foreign ministers' conferences, there were unmistakable signs that Stalin had reconsidered his policy of collaboration with the West.

Before I left the Soviet Union after the war, I went to see Stalin at the Black Sea resort of Sochi. I spent several days there going over with him some of our disagreements. When I argued with him about his unwillingness to cooperate with us he said to me that the Soviet government had decided to go its own way. It became all too clear, from the way he discussed the issues between us, that he had indeed reconsidered the idea of collaboration and meant to press for Communist expansion wherever the opportunity offered. Subsequently the coup in Czechoslovakia, the Berlin Blockade and finally the Korean War demonstrated to the remaining doubters what this meant.

Whatever changes have taken place since I left the Soviet Union, it is clear to me that Khrushchev is still sticking to Stalin's decision for the active political expansion of Communism. At his so-called secret speech to the Twentieth Party Congress Khrushchev severely criticized many of Stalin's internal policies and his attitude both to the Soviet people and to his immediate associates. There is some evidence that that speech also contained a section dealing with Stalin's errors in foreign policy. When I asked Khrushchev if that was so he denied it. However, when I suggested that the outside world as well as the Soviet people and Stalin's subordinates had also suffered from Stalin's arbitrary capriciousness, Khrushchev readily agreed. "Stalin was not blameless in foreign matters," he said.

Nevertheless, in his basic decisions Stalin was correct, Khrushchev made it clear. When I asked whether this included the decision to come to terms with Hitler in 1939, Khrushchev vehemently defended his old chief. He said my question was "cheap." "We knew," he went on, "that France and England were encouraging Hitler to attack Russia. Stalin made the right decision when he agreed to the Ribbentrop-Molotov pact, and what is more we would do the same thing again today." But then he calmed down and added, "Let us not discuss history today, let us talk of the future."

"The state of war with Germany today," he said, "is an anachronism." The occupation of Berlin must be liquidated, and if the West would not agree then the Soviet Union would terminate the occupation alone. It would make a treaty with East Germany and turn over to it the Soviet rights in Berlin and elsewhere. I explained to him that any unilateral action on his part would be extremely dangerous and that Republicans and Democrats are both united behind President Eisenhower in supporting the freedom of the people of West Berlin. "Some of your generals talk of defending your right of access to Berlin with tanks. If you try that your tanks will burn," he said angrily.

"You can rest assured," Khrushchev told me, "that I will agree to no reunification of Germany which does not provide for the socialist [meaning Communist] system. I am equally sure that you do not want a reunification that does not provide for your form of political system." It was obvious to him, therefore, that there could be no agreement on reunification at this time. Hence there was nothing to do but settle the Berlin issue by ending the occupation status, creating a free city of West Berlin and making peace with the two Germanies.

Khrushchev said he found merit in the idea of disengagement in Germany, as some people have proposed. He said that under certain conditions he was prepared to withdraw Soviet troops to within the Soviet frontiers. But he did not elaborate on what those conditions might be.

Turning to the Far East, he again defended Stalin's basic decisions. It was quite true, he said, that Stalin had agreed with Roosevelt to support Chiang Kai-shek; but when the war was over the Soviet Union had other objectives in the East, and when Mao Tse-tung challenged Chiang it would have been absurd to expect Stalin to back Chiang against the Communist.

Although he intimated that dealing with Mao required very delicate diplomacy because the Chinese have their own peculiar way of thinking and acting, he gave no intimation that Moscow's relations with Peking were in any way strained. It may well be that he is sometimes irked by Mao's role as the leading Communist in Asia and occasionally finds it necessary to take initiatives and seek successes in foreign affairs in order to assert his position as the leader of the most powerful Communist state. However, he made it very clear that when China or any other Communist state comes into conflict with the non-Communist world his loyalties are with the former.

He told me that the French politician Mendès-France had suggested to him that China with its exploding birth rate might one day spill over into Siberia in search of food. The idea, he said, was absurd. The Chinese are themselves growing more food, and if they ever needed still more, the Soviet Union would be glad to convert the Siberian forests into arable land and grow enough food to feed the entire Chinese nation.

He chided me for the United States' defense of Formosa and said ominously that if ever the Chinese Communists should seek to assert their rights in Formosa and a third power intervened it would find itself up against the Soviet Union. If the Seventh Fleet intervened, he said, it would be destroyed.

As for the rest of the world. Khrushchev said, the Soviet Union had no pretensions anywhere. It was accused of having designs on the Arab lands, but this was ridiculous. "What do we want from the Middle East? Cotton? We grow our own and better. Oil? We have plenty. Do you want to buy some?" he asked me facetiously.

While he insisted that the Soviet Union only wanted to preserve the status quo, he made it very clear that his idea of the status quo was not the preservation of existing boundaries and balances. An essential element of the world's status today, as Khrushchev sees it, is the Communist march toward world domination. Anything that opposes Communism on the march he considers is altering the status quo and is therefore an act of aggression.

This concept was made even more clear by the Communist drive in Laos after I had left Moscow. When the United States sent a small military training group to Laos, *Pravda* blatantly charged that the United States was committing an act of aggression by helping the Laotians defend themselves against a Communist invasion from North Vietnam.

In only one area did I see some hope of reaching a constructive agreement with Khrushchev—the control and

possible limitation of armaments. In our talks Khrushchev
enjoyed telling me how easily the Soviets could destroy
Paris, London and Bonn. When I asked him if Moscow and
Leningrad were any less vulnerable, he answered, "Leningrad is not Russia any longer. You have seen our Siberian
cities like Irkutsk. They represent Russia's industrial
strength today." Nevertheless, it was clear to me that Mr.
Khrushchev and his military advisers appreciate fully that
for all its alleged ideological superiority the Communist
world is no less vulnerable to H-bombs than the capitalist.
Marshal Malinovsky, the Soviet Defense Minister, during a
long discussion said to me, "Of one thing we can all be sure.
There are already enough nuclear weapons to destroy the
entire world." And when I underlined that this included the
Soviet world, Malinovsky answered, "Undoubtedly."

I think that Mr. Khrushchev is keenly anxious to improve
Soviet living standards. I believe that he looks upon the current Seven-Year Plan as the crowning success of the Communist revolution and a historic turning point in the lives
of the Soviet people. He also considers it a monument
to himself that will mark him in Russian history as one
of his country's great benefactors. However, as I have
indicated elsewhere, he is finding it difficult to attain the
ambitious goals set forth in the plan so long as armaments
are making such heavy demands for scientific genius, technical skill and capital investment. Currently, for example,
armament industries are consuming twenty per cent of the
gross national product—about twice the United States
percentage—which could otherwise go to achieving civilian
production goals.

Frequently during our talks he spoke of his desire to
limit armaments. He expressed his readiness to accept
various forms of controls for that purpose. He said that

though President Eisenhower's aerial-inspection plan was manifestly unfair to the Soviet Union because of the American military bases which girdled his country, he would be willing to accept it as part of an inspection system.

"We want to disarm and cease the cold war," he said repeatedly. "You say you also want to, but we don't seem to be able to agree." He pointed out that he had also suggested international control of communications in order to prevent surprise attack. But the United States had rejected this.

"We do not believe," he added, "that the United States is serious about controls for nuclear weapons."

If Khrushchev could be brought to agree on some limitation of arms with adequate controls, I believe that it would not only reduce the danger of war that is inherent in any arms race; it would not merely reduce the burden of taxes which we must now pay for defense; it would have a third even more profound influence on the future:

Ever since the Revolution it has been a permanent theme of Soviet propaganda that the fortress of Communism is being threatened by the capitalist world. The potential aggressor has changed. For years it was Japan. Later it was Hitler Germany. Today it is the United States. The purpose of this campaign is to stir the Soviet people to greater efforts, to explain the sacrifices they must undergo to build up the heavy industry on which arms production depends, and to justify the Kremlin's claim for the blind obedience and loyalty of the people as a security measure. If, therefore, an agreement on arms limitation can be reached with Khrushchev, it will constitute a tacit admission that the threat of American aggression has diminished. With it the justification for the frenzied pace with which he is driving the Soviet people to work harder will diminish.

Similarly, the need for heavy industry's priority over consumer industries will lessen. Finally, the demand for blind obedience and unquestioning loyalty will be far more difficult to explain.

The information I gathered and the impressions I gained during my recent travels in the Soviet Union and my conversations with its leaders have, I believe, several implications which may be helpful in the consideration of our future attitude toward the U.S.S.R. Here in brief are some of them.

We can no longer afford to be deluded by myths or have our policies muddled by confusion about what is going on in the Soviet Union. We cannot find comfort in any idea that the Communist regime is going to be overthrown or converted to our own beliefs. For the foreseeable future the leaders in the Kremlin are going to be guided by their firm faith in the triumphal spread of their doctrine across the globe. For a long time to come we are going to face this threat everywhere.

On the other hand, I have never believed and do not believe now that war is inevitable in our struggle to thwart the march of Communism. Nor do I think that the present Soviet leaders will bring on war except by miscalculation or mistake.

But we must dismiss as a pleasant daydream any thought of Mr. Khrushchev's peaceful coexistence and apply ourselves to the challenge of all-out competitive coexistence—competition for survival. The Kremlin leaders cannot be diverted from their primary goal of world revolution with a diplomacy of threats and ultimatums. Affirmative action is called for.

Our first and most important job, I believe, is to maintain the vigor and vitality of our own social and economic system. We must speed up our economic growth to make the fullest use of our natural and human resources and to improve American life in all its aspects for all our citizens.

In the second place, we must meet the challenge posed by Soviet advances in science by improving our own system of education and turning out enough qualified scientists and specialists to maintain our leadership in this field, but without for a moment sacrificing our primary aim of developing well-rounded, well-educated individuals.

Until we have reached some agreement on arms limitations with foolproof controls we cannot even consider any relaxation of our effort to maintain our defenses and those of our allies, especially those of the North Atlantic community.

At the same time we must assert vigorous and imaginative leadership to make the North Atlantic Treaty Organization not only a strong military alliance but also a united and productive community which combines our resources for the social and economic advancement of its members and the free world.

We must also meet the challenge Khrushchev has posed in the underdeveloped countries by assisting them more effectively and consistently to build their own economies in freedom. And we must also share our political experience and our sociological advances with them so that their political and social development will keep pace with the industrial growth and help them to find solutions to the serious problems which that growth inevitably creates.

We cannot permit our dealings with the Soviet Union itself, any more than our domestic problems or our relations with our allies, to become fixed, rigid or inactive. The

Soviet Union is not a static society. Its Communist leaders are constantly subject to pressure both economic and social.

I believe that they are playing a losing game in their efforts to maintain thought control. Their old dream of creating a new Soviet man thoroughly indoctrinated with Communist ideology has definitely failed. And Khrushchev, I am convinced, is finding it increasingly difficult to maintain thought control without the police control of Stalin which he has abandoned.

I do not believe that radical changes will take place overnight, but I think that the people's justifiable demands for a greater share in the fruits of the Soviet economy will one day substantially modify the emphasis which the Soviet government has placed on its intense efforts for world Communism, now held to with such fanatical insistence by the present rulers. I also believe that the demand for greater freedom is inherent in all peoples and that it too will make itself felt as the immediate demand for more material needs is met.

These and other pressures will, I think, open up new possibilities for restraining the militancy of the Communist regime. I believe therefore that we should ceaselessly probe every possible avenue of approach to agreements with the Soviet Union rather than reject out of hand every proposal its government makes.

To increase the pressures on the Kremlin we should encourage the legitimate aspirations of the Soviet people for peace, freedom and a reasonable living standard, by multiplying our efforts to break down the barriers to communications through exchange both of people and of information. We should not only encourage American tourists to visit the Soviet Union but we should urge Soviet tourists in equal numbers to visit us. We should expand the exchange of students, teachers, scientists and others and encourage the Soviet Union to participate in continuing international scientific and social research. The contacts established during the International Geophysical Year should not be allowed to die but should be strengthened by continuing association in similar fields, such as world-wide meteorology, oceanography and the problems of outer space. We should also try to induce the Soviets to become permanent participating members of international organizations in the fields of medicine and education.

Take the case of President Eisenhower's trip to the Soviet Union. It is certain to convince some Russians that it is unthinkable that America would ever start a war. It will lead countless others at least to begin to doubt the accuracy of their government's propaganda against us. This will increase the popular pressure on the Kremlin for a return to the friendly relations which existed with us during the war and which the Russian people crave so deeply.

Though Khrushchev has not abandoned the traditional techniques of international Communism, he has now made us a new challenge in a realm we know something about. He has said he will overwhelm us by creating an economic and social system so successful that "other countries will have to follow it." Here is a field in which Americans have excelled for generations. We can only welcome the challenge and spare none of our native genius in meeting it.

The challenge is not alone in the field of economic growth but in all aspects of our social life. It is in education, public health and human rights. It is also in the problems of our rapidly growing metropolitan areas—housing, mass transportation, parks and playgrounds and many others. Many of these tasks require public planning and investment. They are tasks we would accept without the spur of the Soviet Union, but now when they involve our survival in freedom they demand national action.

For my part I have no doubt that in our free institutions we have a wealth of initiative and creative talent to meet these challenges which no totalitarian society can muster.

ABOUT THE AUTHOR

There is no living American who has known Russia over as many years, and has talked with its leaders at such crucial moments in their history, as Averell Harriman. He visited Siberia in 1899 with his father. In 1926, while he was winding up (profitably) a manganese concession in the Caucasus, he talked for four hours with Leon Trotsky. In 1941, President Roosevelt sent him to Moscow with Lord Beaverbrook to negotiate the first war-aid agreement with Stalin, and the next year he went back with Winston Churchill for the first of the momentous talks on strategy which led to the final defeat of Hitler's Germany. From 1943 to 1946 he was Ambassador to the Soviet Union, years in which he saw Stalin more often than did any other foreigner.

Now the former Governor of New York has just returned from a six-week trip during which he traveled 18,000 miles through the country, seeing parts of Central Asia and Siberia which no American had been allowed to visit previously. He also had a series of long conversations with Nikita Khrushchev, with leading government officials and with hundreds of Soviet citizens and workers. This is the first book he has ever written on Russia.

DATE DUE

MAR 2 9 1980			
GAYLORD			PRINTED IN U.S.A.